OXFORD PICTURE DICTIONARY

SECOND EDITION

Tim Collins, Robyn Brinks Lockwood,
Jayme Adelson-Goldstein, Renée Weiss and Norma Shapiro

OXFORD
UNIVERSITY PRESS

198 Madison Avenue
New York, NY 10016 USA

Great Clarendon Street, Oxford OX2 6DP UK

Oxford University Press is a department of the University of Oxford. It furthers the University's objective of excellence in research, scholarship, and education by publishing worldwide in

Oxford   New York
Auckland   Cape Town   Dar es Salaam   Hong Kong   Karachi
Kuala Lumpur   Madrid   Melbourne   Mexico City   Nairobi
New Delhi   Shanghai   Taipei   Toronto

With offices in
Argentina   Austria   Brazil   Chile   Czech Republic   France   Greece
Guatemala   Hungary   Italy   Japan   Poland   Portugal   Singapore
South Korea   Switzerland   Thailand   Turkey   Ukraine   Vietnam

OXFORD and OXFORD ENGLISH are registered trademarks of Oxford University Press.

© Oxford University Press 2009

Database right Oxford University Press (maker)

Executive Publishing Manager: Stephanie Karras
Managing Editor: Sharon Sargent
Associate Development Editor: Hannah Ryu
Art Design Production Director: Susan Sanguily
Design Manager: Maj-Britt Hagsted
Project Manager: Allison Harm
Production Layout Artist: Colleen Ho
Cover Design: Stacy Merlin
Senior Image Editor: Justine Eun
Image Editor: Robin Fadool
Manufacturing Manager: Shanta Persaud
Manufacturing Coordinator: Faye Wang

ISBN: 978 0 19 474023 4

Printed in Hong Kong

10 9 8 7 6 5 4 3 2

Illustrations by: Accurate Art, Inc.: 3, 23, 44, 46, 65; Roger Audette/Wilkinson Studios: 82, 139, 162-163, 181-182, 219-220; Shawn Banner: 51-52, 184-185, 222-223; Nicoletta Barolini: 17-18, 55- 56, 93- 94, 169-170, 207-208; John Batten: 5, 176, 179, 212, 217; Thomas Booth: 27; David Cain: 6, 46, 103, 158, 213; Richard Carbajal/ Deborah Wolfe, Ltd: 4, 43, 62, 138, 175, 177, 214; Laurie Conley: 124-125, 143-144; Bill Dickson/Contact Jupiter: 16, 22, 24, 36-37, 41-42, 61, 63, 92, 99-100, 117-118, 122, 155-156, 158 141, 168, 200-201, 225; Kevin Hopgood: 54, 111, 149, 187; Jo Kurtz: 6, 25, 29, 30, 70-71, 81, 86-87, 101,103, 105-106, 119, 136-137, 174, 193, 196, 213, 215; Scott MacNeill: 19, 38, 57, 76, 95, 114, 133, 152, 171, 190, 209, 228; Tom Newsom: 8, 41, 141, 155-158, 160; Vilma Ortiz: 120; Karen Pletrobono: 46, 80, 84, 155-157, 160, 174; Zina Saunders: 10-11, 48-49, 60-61, 67-68, 119, 136-138, 141, 193-195, 198; Tom Sperling: 23, 25, 27, 32-33, 63, 65, 79, 80-81, 84, 127-128, 165-166; Gary Undercuffler: 99-101, 108-109, 176, 179, 203-204, 212; Anna Veltfort: 9, 28, 47, 66, 85, 104, 123, 142, 161, 180, 199, 218; Bill Waitzman: 35, 73, 130, 206; Nina Wallace: 112-113, 131-132, 150-151, 188-189, 226-227; Patrick J. Welsh: 13-14, 22, 8, 90, 98, 117, 122, 146-147, 193-196, 198, 215.

Chapter icons designed by Von Glitschka/Scott Hull Associates

Cover Art by CUBE/Illustrations Ltd (hummingbird)

Table of Contents

Table of Contents

Table of Contents

Table of Contents

Introduction

Welcome to *Classic Classroom Activities*, a teacher resource book containing 168 reproducible activities that foster meaningful student-to-student interaction and develop cooperative critical thinking and problem-solving skills. The activities, suitable for low- to intermediate-level adult and young adult ESL students, incorporate the topics and vocabulary from *The Oxford Picture Dictionary*. Each activity strengthens students' accuracy and fluency in listening to and speaking English as well as providing opportunities for reading and writing skills at the word and sentence level.

We hope this resource helps you and your students reach your classroom goals with a boost of energy and enjoyment!

1. WHAT ARE THE PRINCIPLES BEHIND CLASSIC CLASSROOM ACTIVITIES?

The content and methodology found in *Classic Classroom Activities* combine both "classic" and innovative approaches and principles in ESL teaching:

▶ **Students benefit from communicative activities in varied group configurations.**
Classic Classroom Activities contains activities where students work individually, in pairs, in small groups, and with the whole class. In addition, many of the activities require students to switch from one grouping to another in order to complete an activity.

▶ **ESL students have varied needs and interests.**
Each activity is self-contained, allowing you to pick and choose the topics and vocabulary most relevant to your students. You may also choose to teach the units sequentially.

▶ **Listening, speaking, reading, and writing, as well as grammar, phonetics, and vocabulary should not be taught in isolation.**
Classic Classroom Activities links essential vocabulary to the four skills. Your students improve their linguistic competency as they work on each activity.

▶ **Visuals help students learn new language.**
The activity pages feature clear, engaging art providing context that supports interesting student-centered tasks. Content-based picture cards (80 in each unit) provide hands-on, manipulative practice.

▶ **Most teachers need activities for multilevel classrooms.**
Classic Classroom Activities devotes a separate section to multilevel applications in the Teacher's Notes. Specific suggestions help teachers who have one or more low-beginning, high-beginning, and/or low-intermediate students. These multilevel adaptations enable you to make the activity easier or more challenging and to vary the degree of student independence.

2. WHAT'S IN THIS BOOK AND HOW IS IT ORGANIZED?

12 Topic-Based Units
The topics and vocabulary utilized in *Classic Classroom Activities* correspond to the 12 thematic units in *The Oxford Picture Dictionary*. These topics feature practical and essential vocabulary that students need to learn for their everyday communicative tasks at school, at work, and at home.

Teacher's Notes
Teacher's Notes provide essential information for setting up, conducting, and extending each of the 13 activity types. Step-by-step instructions for conducting an activity, variations for multilevel classes, and helpful tips are included for each activity.

13 Activity Types
Thirteen unique activities are featured in almost every unit. See the next page for a descriptive chart.

960 Reproducible Picture Cards
Every unit in *Classic Classroom Activities* contains five pages of topic-related picture cards, with 16 cards on each page. The picture cards are categorized into four different activity types, but all of them can be used as flash or study cards.

48 Grammar Activities

Each unit also contains 4 activities that focus on grammar skills and practice. Working with both vocabulary and grammar in context helps students retain what they learn, and by combining pattern practice with realistic language in context, these activities build students' accuracy and fluency.

An Activity Index

The index, on pages 230-232, is organized by activity type, providing quick access to a particular activity's page number.

3. HOW DO I USE CLASSIC CLASSROOM ACTIVITIES?

Before beginning an activity with your class, review the Teacher's Notes for that activity located on pages xiii–xxv. To get started, read the **Activity Objective** to discover the purpose of the activity and the **Before Class** section to learn how to prepare for it. In addition, read the information in the upper right-hand corner of the page for how to group students, how much time to allow for each activity, and which levels are most suited for a particular activity.

Next, read the directions for either **Quick Start** or **Step by Step**. **Quick Start** condenses the preview, presentation, and practice stages of a classroom activity into three easy steps while **Step by Step** contains more detailed, numbered steps for the activity. The **Hot Tip** offers suggestions for troubleshooting problems that may arise during the activity and for making the activity simpler or more challenging.

Finally, **For Multilevel Classes** contains specific suggestions to enable you to customize the activity to your students' language levels.

4. WHAT TYPES OF ACTIVITIES ARE IN THE BOOK?

The chart below lists the activity types found in *Classic Classroom Activities*. These activities are appropriate for all levels with the exception of Role Play and Take a Stand, which work best with high-beginning or low-intermediate students.

Each activity is self-contained, so you may randomly choose any activity in the unit or you can work sequentially. Within each unit, the activities are generally ordered from lower level to more challenging. For example, you will always find Flash Cards as the first activity in each unit and Take a Stand as the last.

Activity	Grouping	Description
Flash Cards	Pairs	Student pairs take turns showing each other a card and saying the pictured item.
Guess What? Cards	Small Groups	Students take turns describing a picture card to group members who then guess the pictured vocabulary item.
Charades Cards	Small Groups	Students take turns acting out the action depicted on a picture card. Group members identify and say the action in the verb tense being practiced.
Twin Grids	Pairs	Student pairs work together to make identical picture grids without looking at each others' grids.
Round Table Label	Small Groups	Students work in groups to label pictured vocabulary items.
Drawing Dictation	Pairs	Student pairs take turns describing pictures and drawing them according to their partners' directions.
Sentence Maker	Small Groups	Students work in groups to create 10 sentences or questions using word cards.

Picture Differences	Pairs	Student pairs examine two almost identical scenes to find 10 differences between them.
Survey	Whole Class	Students ask and answer questions about personal preferences and write sentences about classmates' answers.
Group Writing	Small Groups	Students work in groups to write sentences to complete a story about a picture.
Information Exchange	Pairs	Student pairs work to find out missing information on their own activity sheets.
Role Play	Small Groups	Students work in groups to read a topic-related play and act it out.
Take a Stand	Pairs	Student pairs analyze statements and decide which of two positions a statement supports. Students write sentences about their opinions.

5. HOW ELSE CAN I USE THE PICTURE CARDS?

There are four picture card activities in each unit: Flash Cards, Guess What? Cards, Charades Cards, and Twin Grids. Step-by-step directions for these activities can be found on pages xiii–xvi. There are many other ways to use the same picture cards for additional vocabulary practice. Here are some suggestions:

▶ **Picture Card Dictionary**
Cut off the word lists, distribute one page of picture cards per student, and have students work together to label the pictures. Once they have completed several pages, they can assemble their own picture dictionaries.

▶ **Spelling Tests**
Cut off the word lists, distribute one page of picture cards per student, and use the picture cards as a spelling test.

▶ **Flyswatter Review Game**
Make transparencies of picture cards, cut apart the cards, and arrange 8–10 pictures on an overhead projector. Divide the class into two teams lined-up on either side of the room. Give the first person on each team a flyswatter. Say a sentence containing one of the words. The first student to hit the correct (projected) picture earns a point for his/her team. Have the student pass the flyswatter to the next team member and continue the game. Every few turns, change and/or rearrange the pictures.

▶ **Card-Exchange Mixer**
Cut apart picture cards and give one card to each student. Write a question skeleton on the board that will work with any of the pictured items, e.g., *Do you like _____? Have you ever _____?, etc.* Have students find a partner, ask and answer the question using the picture card they are holding, exchange cards, and then circulate around the room to find a new partner.

▶ **Matching Mixer**
Copy a set of picture cards onto two different colors of card stock. Pass out cards of one color to half of the students and the other color to the other half. Be sure that most of the students will have a "partner" on the other side, i.e., the same picture on a different colored card. Keep the extras in a pile. Have students find their partners by following a skeleton prompt on the board, e.g., *A: Can I borrow your _____? B: I don't have a _____. or I have a _____. or I think (student name) has a _____.* When students find their partners, have them turn in their cards. Continue until all cards are used.

6. DO YOU HAVE TIPS FOR ASSEMBLING AND STORING MATERIALS?

Reproducible Activity Sheets

Before beginning any activity, make sure you check the **Before Class** section at the top of the Teacher's Notes. Do this before you start duplicating a class set of activity sheets. Many of the activities are for pairs or groups and do not require individual copies of the materials. Also, gather all the materials you will need, such as manila folders and scissors, for the activity.

Picture Cards

How you assemble and organize your picture cards depends greatly on how you choose to use them in your classroom. You can have students color the picture card pages and then laminate them. You can duplicate entire class sets of Picture Card pages and store them, with or without the accompanying Word List. You can store the cut-apart picture cards in class sets of envelopes or have students create their own storage pockets by stapling half-sheets of construction paper to both sides of manila folders. These pocket folders of manipulatives can then be taken home for student practice or kept in a file box in the classroom.

Props

The Role Play activity calls for props or real objects to help set the stage and bring the activity to life. You can provide these materials (storing them in the classroom if you have space) or consider asking students to bring something in. Telling students about the activity a few days beforehand will build anticipation and provide time to allow them to collect what they need to bring from home.

7. HOW DO I FACILITATE THE ACTIVITIES?

Checking Comprehension

Classic Classroom Activities is not designed to teach the meaning of new vocabulary. It is crucial that students understand both the vocabulary on the activity page and the directions for the activity. Every activity page gives *The Oxford Picture Dictionary* page number(s) for the vocabulary used in the activity. If necessary, review and practice these words with your students before you begin the activity. To ensure that the activities run smoothly, all the Teacher's Notes contain specific techniques for checking your students' comprehension of the directions.

Grouping Strategies

The act of grouping students in pairs or small groups is a communicative activity in itself. The way students are grouped facilitates their speaking practice by reducing first-language interference and non-participation. As much as possible, have students work in mixed-language, mixed-ability, and/or mixed-gender groups.

Pair Groups

Since many activities involve student pairs, it is a good idea to encourage students to work with as many different people as possible. You can manipulate the distribution of student pairs by using playing cards and picture cards, giving specific cards to higher-level students, one language group, or one gender. You can also:

- Hand out playing cards and have students with the same numbers find each other to form pairs.
- Distribute picture cards to half the class and word cards you've created to the other half. Have students match pictures with words to form pairs.

Small Groups

Small group activities are most successful when group members have certain responsibilities. Responsibilities could include recorder, timekeeper, reporter, reader, English monitor, and observer. Alternate allowing students to form their own groups, assigning students into specific groups, or forming groups at random. To form groups:

- Take some time to mentally identify the homogeneous groups in your class (languages, ages, levels). Distribute one kind of card to each group. (All Spanish speakers get #1 or A, all Armenian speakers get #2 or B, etc.) Have students form groups of four different numbers or letters.
- Make name cards ahead of time and place them on the desks for "pre-assigned" groups. This works well if you have regularly attending students.
- Cut magazine pictures into four separate

pieces, randomly distribute them, and have students "reassemble" the pictures to form their groups.

Monitoring

Your most important role during every activity is being aware of what's going on while students are doing the activity. This is the best time to assess how the activity is progressing and if it is meeting your students' needs. Walk around as unobtrusively as possible, making mental or actual notes of where students are having difficulty. Listen for grammar and pronunciation problems and "jump in" if students need you.

Time Limits and Quiet Signals

Students need to know the parameters of a communicative task, including the time it takes to complete it. The use of a quiet signal to get the attention of the class helps students shift gears between the stages of an activity. Try these "attention grabbers" and make sure to vary them so they retain their punch: turn the lights off, ring a bell, blow a whistle, raise your hand, wave a flag.

8. HOW CAN I USE THE OVERHEAD PROJECTOR (OHP)?

Teachers fortunate enough to have OHPs in their classrooms will find overhead transparencies very helpful. Here are some suggestions for using transparencies:

- Make a transparency of the activity and use it before distributing your class set. By masking sections with blank paper, you can focus students' attention on just a portion of the sheet while you set up the activity. You or a student volunteer can write directly on the transparency to model the activity.

- Play "Concentration" with the whole class to reinforce vocabulary. Draw and make a transparency of a 16-square grid. Write the letters A-D across the top of the grid and number the boxes 1–4 down the left of the grid. Make a transparency of a selected picture card page and cut apart the pictures. Choose 8 pictures and place them in the boxes in the top two rows of the grid. In the remaining squares, write the corresponding words. Using 16 small squares of paper, mask each of the

squares on the entire grid. Have students take turns calling out two squares (A2 and B4), trying to match the picture and the word.

- Transparencies of *The Oxford Picture Dictionary* pages are available and are useful for reviewing an activity's target vocabulary and/or providing additional vocabulary practice.

Activity Objective: Student pairs take turns showing each other a card and saying the pictured item.

Before Class: Duplicate the selected Flash Cards activity sheet and collect scissors for each pair. Duplicate and enlarge one Flash Card or draw a simple object on a piece of paper.

Pairs

20 minutes

Low-Beginning
High-Beginning
Low-Intermediate

Quick Start

Ready:	Set:	Go:
Ready: Duplicate and enlarge a Flash Card or draw a simple object on a piece of paper that the whole class can see. Write the pictured item on the back of the card or piece of paper. Ask students to say the pictured item. Check students' answers by showing them the back of the card.	**Set:** Have students form pairs. Distribute the activity sheets, scissors, and review the directions. Make sure students understand they will share one set of cards. Have students use the Word List to write the corresponding word(s) on the back of each picture and then cut apart the cards.	**Go:** Have students hold up a flash card for their partner to say. Partners take turns. The activity ends when all cards have been identified and said correctly.

Step by Step

1. Copy and enlarge a Flash Card or draw a simple object on a piece of paper that the whole class can see. Write the pictured item on the back of the card or piece of paper. Hold it up and ask students to say the pictured item. Check students' answers by showing them the back of the card.

2. Hold up an activity sheet, and tell students that they will work with a partner to identify and say the pictured items. Distribute the activity sheets and scissors.

3. In pairs, have students use the Word List to write the words on the back of the cards. Then have them put the Word List aside.

4. Have students cut apart the cards and stack them face-up. Tell students they will take turns pulling cards off the stack.

5. Review the directions and check for comprehension by asking: *Do you use the Word List*

to write the words on the back of the cards? [yes] *Do you tell your partner what your picture card is?* [no]

6. Get pairs started by having one student pull a card from the top of the stack and show the picture to his/her partner. The partner says the pictured vocabulary, and the student holding the card checks the partner by looking at the back of the card. If the card was not said correctly, the student should put it back at the bottom of the stack.

7. Have pairs continue identifying and saying the pictured items. Monitor student practice by walking around to check students' progress and to help with language difficulties.

8. Have students continue until all the cards have been identified correctly.

Hot Tip *Have higher-level students pair with lower-level ones so students can help each other.*

For Multilevel Classes

Low-Beginning: Remove the Word List before duplicating one set of Flash Cards for each student. Have these students write the words on the back of the correct cards as you dictate the spelling.

High-Beginning: Have these students complete the activity as outlined above.

Low-Intermediate: Have these students say and spell out each picture card.

Activity Objective: Students take turns verbally describing a picture card to group members who then guess the pictured vocabulary item.

Before Class: Duplicate the selected Guess What? Cards activity sheet and collect scissors for each group of 4. Cut the Word List apart from the activity sheets. Look over the activity sheet to determine vocabulary students may need to review.

Groups of 4

35 minutes

**Low-Beginning
High-Beginning
Low-Intermediate**

Quick Start

Ready: Have students form groups of 4. Give each group a copy of the Word List. As a class, review the definitions of the words or phrases on the Word List. Cut apart a card from the activity sheet. Tell students you will describe the pictured item and they must guess what it is. Then describe the picture, but do not use the target word or phrase in your description.

Set: Distribute the activity sheets, scissors, and review the directions. Have students cut apart the cards. Model the activity by having a student in one group look at a card and describe it to the other group members. Remind students not to use the target word or phrase in their descriptions. Have the student give the card to the first group member who answers correctly.

Go: Have students take turns describing cards and guessing the vocabulary. The activity ends when all cards have been guessed correctly.

Step by Step

1. Have students form groups of 4. Give each group a copy of the Word List. As a class, review the definitions of the words or phrases on the Word List.

2. Cut apart a card from the activity sheet. Tell students you will describe the picture and they must guess what it is. Then describe it, but do not use the target word or phrase in your description. Encourage students to answer. Give the picture card to the first student who answers correctly.

3. Distribute the activity sheets and scissors to each group. Have students cut apart the cards and stack them face-down.

4. Review the directions and check for comprehension by asking: *Can you use any part of the word in your description?* [no] *Does the first student to answer correctly keep the card?* [yes]

5. Model the activity by having a student in one group look at a card and describe it to the other group members. Have the student give the card to the first group member who answers correctly.

6. Have students take turns describing and guessing. Monitor student practice by walking around to help with descriptions and to answer any questions.

7. Have students continue until all cards have been identified and spelled correctly. Find out which student in each *group* got the most cards and which student in the *class* got the most cards.

Hot Tip *After the activity, gather the cards for reuse in future classes. Provide an envelope for each set of cards.*

For Multilevel Classes

Low-Beginning: As you review the Word List before the activity, write brief definitions or key words for each card on the board to help these students. Then have students complete the activity as outlined above.

High-Beginning: Have these students complete the activity as outlined above.

Low-Intermediate: Have these students use the words on the cards to write sentences.

Activity Objective: Students take turns acting out the action depicted on a picture card. Group members identify and say the action in the verb tense being practiced.

Before Class: Duplicate the selected Charades Cards activity sheet and collect scissors for each group of 4.

Quick Start

Ready: Have a volunteer come up and ask him/her to pantomime *mow the lawn* for the class. Then in the verb tense being practiced, ask students what their classmate is doing. For example, if the activity practices past tense, ask: *What did he/she do?* Encourage students to call out sentence answers. Write the correct sentence on the board: *He/She mowed the lawn.*	**Set:** Have students form groups of 4. Distribute the activity sheets, scissors, and review the directions. Have students cut apart the cards and put aside the Word List. Model the activity by having a student in one group look at a card and pantomime it to the other group members. Have another student write the correct sentence answer.	**Go:** Have students take turns pantomiming the action on the cards. The first student pantomimes; the second student asks about that classmate using the prompt provided in the directions. The other two students answer using a sentence. The second student writes what they say. The activity ends when students have correctly identified all of the actions.

Step by Step

1. Have a volunteer come up and ask him/her to pantomime *mow the lawn* for the class. Then in the verb tense being practiced, ask students what their classmate is doing. For example, if the activity practices past tense, ask: *What did he/she do?* Encourage students to call out sentence answers. If necessary, have the volunteer repeat the pantomime.

2. When students call out the right answer, write the correct sentence on the board: *He/She mowed the lawn.*

3. Have students form groups of 4 and assign a letter (A, B, C, or D) to each person.

4. Give each Student A an activity sheet and have them remove the Word List to put it aside. Have students cut apart the cards and stack them face-down.

5. Review the directions and check for comprehension by asking: *Do you say anything while you are acting?* [no] *Does the question and answer use the same verb tense?* [yes]

6. Get the groups started by having each Student A draw a card, verify the action using the Word List, and pantomime it. Next, Student B asks Student C and D what Student A is doing using the prompt provided in the directions. Student B writes down what they say. Students should work together to conjugate the verb correctly and form a sentence. After the first card is finished, have the members switch roles.

7. Have students continue until all the cards have been correctly identified. Allow students enough time to correct any errors you find as you circulate.

8. Have groups turn in their cards and read their sentences out loud.

Hot Tip *Encourage students to have fun and not worry about their performance. The goal is not to be a good actor but to practice vocabulary.*

For Multilevel Classes

Low-Beginning: Have these students work together to name the action and spell out the verb or verb phrase as listed in the Word List.

High-Beginning: Have these students complete the activity as outlined above.

Low-Intermediate: Have these students write sentences with the actions in an additional verb tense.

Activity Objective: Student pairs work together to make identical picture grids without looking at each others' grids.

Before Class: Duplicate the selected Twin Grid and Twin Grid Cards activity sheets for each student. Collect scissors and half a class set of manila folders. Make simplified versions of three of the picture cards on large pieces of paper.

Pairs

30 minutes

Low-Beginning
High-Beginning
Low-Intermediate

Quick Start

Ready: Draw the top row of the activity grid on the board. Take a card sheet and cut apart the three cards you made large versions of. Display the large versions and have students name the vocabulary. Then have students form pairs, and distribute the activity sheets, scissors, and manila folders. Have students cut apart the picture cards and place them face-up next to their grid.

Set: Model the activity. As students watch, place the three picture cards on the top row of your grid. Then give a student volunteer the corresponding large cards. Tell the volunteer where to put the cards on the grid on the board by making sentences using the cards and the grid squares. Have the volunteer tape the cards to the correct grid squares. Then ask: *Are the grids the same?*

Go: Assign A/B roles to each pair. Have the A students put cards on their grids and then tell B students where to put the same cards on their grids. When they finish, have them compare grids to check if they are the same. Then have students switch roles and repeat the activity.

Step by Step

1. Draw the top row of the activity grid on the board. Take a card sheet and cut apart the three cards you made large versions of. Display the large cards and have students name the vocabulary.

2. Have students form pairs, and distribute the activity sheets, scissors, and manila folders. Have students cut apart the picture cards and place them face-up next to their grid. Tell students to put aside the Word List for use during the activity.

3. Model the activity. As students watch, place the three picture cards on the top row of your grid. Then give a student volunteer the corresponding large cards. Tell the volunteer where to put the cards on the grid on the board by making sentences using the cards and the grid squares. (For example, a *sunny day* picture on the *today* square makes *It's going to be sunny today.*) Encourage the student to clarify. *Did you say it's going to be sunny today?*

4. Have the volunteer tape the pictures to the correct grid squares. When finished, compare your grids and make sure they are the same.

5. Review the directions and check for comprehension by asking: *Do you show your partner your grid?* [no] *Do you put one picture on each square?* [yes].

6. Assign A/B roles to each pair. Have partners set up the folders between themselves as screens. Remind students that they cannot look at each other's grids.

7. Have the A students place their cards and then tell sentences to the B students so the grids look the same. Tell students to use the language model in the directions. Set a time limit and have students begin working. Encourage students to use the Word List to check their sentences.

8. When partners have finished, have them compare grids to see if they are the same. If they are not, have students try again. If they are the same, have students switch roles and repeat the activity.

Hot Tip *Assign higher-level students to the A role so that they speak first.*

For Multilevel Classes

Low-Beginning: Number each square on grid. Have partners say the number and the picture card on it. A: *One—sunny.* B: *Sunny?* A: *Yes.*

High-Beginning: Have these students complete the activity as outlined above.

Low-Intermediate: Write a more complex dialogue on the board and have these students use it during the activity. A: *What's the weather like today?* B: *It's going to be sunny.* A: *Sunny?* B: *Yes.*

Activity Objective: Students work in groups to label pictured vocabulary items.

Before Class: Duplicate the selected Round Table Label activity sheet for each group of 3.

Quick Start

Ready: Draw two easily identifiable items on the board. For example, draw a shirt and a pair of pants. Label the shirt correctly. Label the pants incorrectly. Ask students to check and correct your work. When they tell you how to label the pants correctly, ask them how to spell it. Then write the correct label on the board.	**Set:** Have students form groups of 3. Distribute the activity sheets and review the directions. Make sure students understand that all members of the group will share the same activity sheet. Model the activity by having one group pass the sheet from one student to the next, each writing their names at the top.	**Go:** Have one student label one item on the activity sheet before handing it to the next. Students should help each other, but only the student with the paper should write on it. After all items are labeled, students look at the *Dictionary* to check their work. The activity ends when all items are labeled correctly.

Step by Step

1. Draw two easily identifiable items on the board. For example, draw a shirt and a pair of pants. Label the shirt correctly. Label the pants incorrectly. Ask students to check and correct your work. When they tell you how to label the pants correctly, ask them how to spell it. Then write the correct label on the board.

2. Hold up an activity sheet. Tell students they will be working in groups of 3, taking turns labeling items on the sheet. Make sure students understand they are allowed to help each other complete the activity.

3. Have students form groups of 3 and assign a number, 1–3, to each person. Give each #1 a duplicate of the activity sheet.

4. Review the directions and check for comprehension by asking: *Do you use your* Dictionary *to label the items?* [no] *Do you pass the paper to the next person after you have labeled an item?* [yes] *Do you use your* Dictionary *to check your spelling after all items are labeled?* [yes]

5. Have #1s label one item. Encourage group members to help. Walk around and assist as necessary.

6. After #1s finish, have them pass the sheet to #2s. Have groups continue labeling items and passing the sheet around. Monitor student progress by walking around to make sure students are helping each other name the items and spell the words correctly.

7. Allow enough time for groups to check their answers against the *Dictionary* after they complete the activity sheet. Have them correct any mistakes.

8. Do the **What's Next** activity with the class.

Hot Tip *Encourage students to sit close together in circles so they can work together and pass the activity sheet easily without disturbing other groups.*

For Multilevel Classes

Low-Beginning: Duplicate the activity sheet onto an overhead transparency and label the scene as a class.

High-Beginning: Have these students complete the activity as outlined above.

Low-Intermediate: Complete the activity sheet and then take turns writing sentences about the labeled items.

Activity Objective: Student pairs take turns describing pictures and drawing them according to their partners' directions.

Before Class: Duplicate half a class set of each page of the selected Drawing Dictation activity sheets and collect half a class set of manila folders. Look over the activity sheets to determine vocabulary students may need to review.

Pairs

30 minutes

Low-Beginning
High-Beginning
Low-Intermediate

Quick Start

Ready: Place several classroom objects on a table and draw an empty table on the board. Ask students to describe the items on the table and their locations. As they describe, draw the items on the board. Model the language and clarification questions by asking questions.	**Set:** Distribute the activity sheets and manila folders. Have students with A sheets find partners with B sheets and have partners set up the folders as screens. Review the directions and the clarification questions. Model the activity by having a student pair describe and draw one item on the activity sheet.	**Go:** Have students complete the first part of the activity. When students are ready, have them switch roles and complete the second part of the activity. When both pictures are complete, have pairs remove the screens and compare their work.

Step by Step

1. Place several classroom objects on a table and draw an empty table on the board. Ask students to describe the items on the table and their locations. As they describe, draw the items on the board. Model the language and clarification questions. *Where did you say it was? Is it on the left or right?*

2. Tell students they will take turns describing and drawing different pictures with their partners.

3. Distribute the activity sheets and manila folders. Have students with A activity sheets find partners with B activity sheets and have partners set up the folders between themselves as screens.

4. Review the directions and check for comprehension by asking: *Do you answer your partner's questions?* [yes] *Do you write the names of the items in the picture?* [no]

5. Have one pair demonstrate the activity for the class. One student describes an item in the drawing, while the other listens and draws it.

6. Have students complete the first part of the activity. When students are ready, have them switch roles and complete the second part of the activity. Monitor student practice by walking around to check on students' progress and to help with clarifying questions.

7. Have students check their completed drawings by removing the screens and comparing them. Have a few pairs share their drawings with the class.

8. Do the **What's Next?** activity with the class.

Hot Tip *A perfect drawing is not the goal. Distributing markers or colored pencils may "loosen up" students and encourage them to have fun.*

For Multilevel Classes

Low-Beginning: Have these students use only the A activity sheet and draw the items the teacher describes. If time allows, repeat with the B activity sheet.

High-Beginning: Have these students complete the activity as outlined above.

Low-Intermediate: Have these students describe the items to their partners without saying the target word. *You drink coffee or tea from this. Draw it on the left side of the table.* [cup]

Activity Objective: Students work in groups to create 10 sentences or questions using word cards.

Before Class: Duplicate the selected Sentence Maker activity sheet and collect scissors for each group.

Quick Start

Ready: Draw six sample cards on the board. For example, *HOME, HE, IS, GOING, ?,* and . Ask students to create one sentence and one question using the cards. When they give the answers *He is going home.* and *Is he going home?*, write them on the board.	**Set:** Have students form groups of 4 or 5. Distribute activity sheets, scissors, and review the directions. Have students cut apart the word cards and select a Recorder for their group. Make sure students understand that all members of the group will share the same activity sheet.	**Go:** Have students work together in groups to create 10 sentences or questions using the cards. Students dictate sentences and questions to the Recorder who writes them down as they are made. Set a time limit of 10 minutes. When time is called, have the Recorders read all the sentences and questions to their group.

Step by Step

1. Draw six sample cards on the board. For example, *HOME, HE, IS, GOING, ?,* and . Ask students to create one sentence and one question using the cards. When they give the answers *He is going home.* and *Is he going home?*, write them on the board.

2. Hold up an activity sheet. Tell students they will work with a group to create sentences and questions using word and punctuation cards.

3. Have students form groups of 4 or 5 and ask each group to select a Recorder to write their sentences.

4. Distribute activity sheets and scissors, and have students cut apart the cards.

5. Review the directions and check for comprehension by asking: *Do you write on the cards?* [no] *Do you make more than one sentence?* [yes] *Does the recorder write the answers?* [yes]

6. Have groups start by creating one sentence for the Recorder to write. Encourage the group members to work together. Walk around the room and assist as necessary.

7. After the groups finish one sentence, set the 10-minute time limit. Have students continue creating and recording their sentences and questions. Monitor student progress by walking around to check students' sentences.

8. Stop the students after time has expired. Have the recorders read all the sentences and questions to their group.

9. Do the **What's Next** activity with the class.

Hot Tip *Review English word order and punctuation before students begin the activity.*

For Multilevel Classes

Low-Beginning: Duplicate the activity sheet onto an overhead transparency and create sentences as a class.

High-Beginning: Have these students complete the activity as detailed.

Low-Intermediate: Have these students write answers to the questions they wrote.

Activity Objective: Student pairs examine two almost identical scenes to find 10 differences between them.

Before Class: Duplicate half a class set of each page of the selected Picture Differences activity sheets. Look over them to determine vocabulary students may need to review.

Quick Start

Ready: Draw two pictures on the board that are the same but have one difference. For example, draw a hand with a ring and draw a hand without a ring. Ask students: *What's the difference?* Write the response under each picture on the board.	**Set:** Distribute activity sheets and review the directions. Have students with A sheets find partners with B sheets. Have students find and point to the sample difference on their activity sheets. Clarify that the difference is written on both students' charts.	**Go:** Have pairs look at their pictures together, search for the differences, and complete their own charts. The activity ends when all 10 picture differences have been discovered.

Step by Step

1. Draw two pictures on the board that are the same but have one difference. For example, draw a hand with a ring and a hand without a ring. Ask students: *What's the difference?* After students answer, write the responses on the board in two columns. *The hand has a ring. The hand doesn't have a ring.*

2. Distribute the activity sheets. Have students with A sheets find partners with B sheets. Tell the students that each partner has a paper with an almost identical scene. Explain that they will look together at both pictures to find and record 10 differences.

3. Review the directions and check for comprehension by asking: *Do you look at each other's pictures?* [yes] *Do you write your answers on only one chart?* [no]

4. Have students cover the charts on the bottom of their activity sheets. Ask the A students to locate the sample item by asking questions such

as: *Do you see a laundry basket? Where is it?* Ask B students the same questions. Ask the students to state the difference in sentences. Write the sentences on the board under A and B.

5. Have pairs examine their pictures, discuss the differences, and write them in the chart. Monitor student progress by walking around and helping with any language difficulties.

6. After students finish recording their answers, have students use their *Dictionary* to check their spelling.

7. When all pairs finish, go over the results with the class. Elicit the picture differences they have found and write them on the board.

8. Do the **What's Next?** activity with the class.

Hot Tip *Make transparencies of the A and B sheets and have volunteers circle the picture differences as you review students' answers.*

For Multilevel Classes

Low-Beginning: Have these students work with the teacher to find the picture differences.

High-Beginning: Have these students complete the activity as outlined above.

Low-Intermediate: Using a screen, partners find and record the differences without looking at each other's pictures. They must talk about the differences instead.

Activity Objective: Students ask and answer questions about personal preferences and write sentences about classmates' answers.

Before Class: Duplicate the selected Survey activity sheet for each student. Look over the activity sheet to determine vocabulary students may need to review.

Whole Class

35 minutes

Low-Beginning
High-Beginning
Low-Intermediate

Quick Start

Ready: Draw a simplified survey chart on the board that includes this preference question: *Do you prefer coffee or tea?* Ask it out loud and answer it yourself by checking your choice under the "My Answers" column. Ask for 5 volunteers. Write their names in the column heads. Then ask the students the same question. Indicate students' choices with a check on the chart.	**Set:** Distribute the activity sheet and review the directions. Model the activity. Have a new student volunteer read and answer the first survey question. Then have the student walk around and ask 5 other students the question. Have the volunteer check all of the students' choices on his/her chart.	**Go:** Have students first answer all the survey question themselves. Then have them walk around the room and survey 5 students to complete their charts. When finished, ask students to use their answers to write sentences about each classmate. Have students work in pairs to read their sentences out loud.

Step by Step

1. Draw a simplified survey chart on the board that includes this preference question: *Do you prefer coffee or tea?* Ask it out loud and answer it yourself by checking your choice under the "My Answers" column.

2. Ask for 5 volunteers. Write their names in the column heads. Then ask the students the same question. Indicate students' choices with a check on the chart.

3. Distribute activity sheets and model the activity. Have a new student volunteer read and answer the first survey question. Then have the student walk around and ask 5 other students the question. Have the volunteer check all of the students' choices on his/her chart.

4. Review the directions and check for comprehension by asking: *Do you first answer all the questions yourself?* [yes] *Do you work together to write sentences?* [no]

5. Have students answer all the survey questions themselves. Then have them walk around the room and survey 5 other students to complete their charts. Walk around to make sure students are marking responses correctly.

6. When students are done, have them return to their seats and use their answers to write sentences about each classmate they interviewed. Monitor student writing by walking around.

7. When students are ready, have them form pairs to read their sentences out loud and compare them. Ask selected students to read their sentences out loud to the class.

8. Do the **What's Next?** activity with the class.

Hot Tip *Some students may not like either of the two options. Tell them for the sake of the activity, they must still make a choice.*

For Multilevel Classes

Low-Beginning: Have these students survey one another in groups of 6, remaining seated together to complete the survey. Then have them work together to write sentences using the results.

High-Beginning: Have these students complete the activity as outlined above.

Low-Intermediate: Before these students begin, help them add 3 more questions to the survey.

Activity Objective: Students work in groups to write sentences to complete a story about a picture.

Before Class: Duplicate the selected Group Writing activity sheet for each group. Look over the activity sheet to determine vocabulary students may need to review.

Groups of 3

25 minutes

Low-Beginning
High-Beginning
Low-Intermediate

Quick Start

Ready: Draw a simple picture on the board. For example, draw a person entering a bank. Write a sentence that could be the first line of a story about the picture. *Jason went to the bank yesterday.* Ask a student volunteer to write the next sentence. Continue letting volunteers add sentences to create a story.

Set: Have students form groups of 3. Distribute the activity sheets and review the directions. Make sure students understand that all members of the group will share the same activity sheet. Model the activity by having one group pass the sheet from one student to the next, each writing their names at the top.

Go: Ask one student in each group to read the first sentence out loud, write the second sentence, and then hand the sheet to the next group member. Students should help each other, but only the student with the paper should write on it. After all lines are completed, students look at the *Dictionary* to check their work.

Step by Step

1. Draw a simple picture on the board. For example, draw a person entering a bank. Write a sentence that could be the first line of a story about the picture. *Jason went to the bank yesterday.*

2. Ask a student volunteer to write the next sentence. Continue letting volunteers add sentences to create a story.

3. Hold up an activity sheet. Tell students they will be working in groups, taking turns writing sentences to complete a story. Make sure students understand they are allowed to help each other write sentences.

4. Have students form groups of 3 and assign a number, 1–3, to each person. Give each #1 a duplicate of the activity sheet. Allow a few minutes for students to study the picture and read the first line of the story.

5. Review the directions and check for comprehension by asking: *Do you write all the sentences by yourself?* [no] *Do the sentences tell a story about the picture?* [yes]

6. Have #1s write the second sentence. Encourage group members to help. After #1s finish, have them pass the sheet to #2s. Have groups continue writing sentences and passing the sheet around. Monitor student progress by walking around to check students' sentences.

7. Allow enough time for groups to check their answers against the *Dictionary* after they complete the story. Have them correct any spelling mistakes.

8. Do the **What's Next** activity with the class.

Hot Tip *Review word order and simple sentence patterns that students can use to write their stories.*

For Multilevel Classes

Low-Beginning: Schedule time to review and write the vocabulary that these students will need to write sentences.

High-Beginning: Have these students complete the activity as outlined above.

Low-Intermediate: Have these students write a story about themselves based on the picture. Ask questions like: *Have you ever been in a situation like the person(s) in the picture? Do you like or dislike what the person is doing?*

Activity Objective: Student pairs work to find out missing information on their own activity sheets.

Before Class: Duplicate half a class set of each page of the selected Information Exchange activity sheets and collect half a class set of manila folders.

Quick Start

Ready: Write a sample sentence on the board leaving blanks for information students need to fill in. For example: *A day has _____ hours and an hour has _____ minutes.* Ask students what questions they need to ask to find out the missing information. *How many hours are in a day? How many minutes are in an hour?*	**Set:** Have students form pairs. Distribute activity sheets, manila folders, and review the directions. Have students set the folder up as screens. Model a sample question from the A and B sheets with the class.	**Go:** Have students ask each other questions to fill in the blanks on their activity sheets. When they have filled in all the missing information, give students time to check their accuracy by comparing their sheets.

Step by Step

1. Review the vocabulary from the relevant *Dictionary* pages as necessary. Write a sample sentence on the board leaving blanks for the information students need to fill in. For example: *A day has _____ hours and an hour has _____ minutes.* Ask students what questions they need to ask to find out the missing information. *How many hours are in a day? How many minutes are in an hour?*

2. Present questions that the students can use to clarify answers. *Did you say 24 or 25? How many minutes was that? Can you repeat that?*

3. Distribute the activity sheets and manila folders. Have students with A activity sheets find partners with B activity sheets and have partners set up the folders between themselves as screens.

4. Review the directions and check for comprehension by asking: *Do you show your partner your activity sheet?* [no] *Do you ask questions about the blanks on your activity sheet?* [yes]

5. Have one student pair demonstrate the activity for the class by having A ask B a question and having A fill in the answer on the A sheet.

6. Have students ask and answer questions to complete their activity sheets. Monitor student practice by walking around to check on students' progress and help with clarification questions.

7. When finished, have students check their accuracy by comparing their sheets.

8. Do the **What's Next** activity with the class.

Hot Tip *Pair students with partners whose native language is different from theirs to encourage the use of English.*

For Multilevel Classes

Low-Beginning: Have these students use only the A activity sheet and fill in missing information as the teacher dictates.

High-Beginning: Have these students complete the activity as outlined above.

Low-Intermediate: Complete the activity, and then have these students work together to create an original recipe, schedule, or brochure using the vocabulary in the activity.

Activity Objective: Students work in groups to read a topic-related play and act it out.

Before Class: Duplicate the selected Role Play activity sheet for each student. Look at the script to determine the target vocabulary required for the activity. Look at the props to determine the items you need to collect.

Groups of 3 or 4

60 minutes

High-Beginning
Low-Intermediate

Quick Start

Ready: Write the scene and characters on the board and display the props. Have students make predictions about conversations they might hear.	**Set:** Have students form groups of 3 or 4 (as required by the Role Play script). Distribute the activity sheets and props. Review the directions and have students practice saying the first two lines of the script.	**Go:** Have students in groups decide which character is speaking each line and add more lines to the script. Have students choose a character, practice the lines, and act out the Role Play. When groups are ready, have them act out their plays for the class.

Step by Step

1. Write the Role Play scene and characters on the board. Display the props and have the students name each one. Use the scene, the characters, and the props to help students make predictions about conversations they might hear. Review the target vocabulary students may need for the activity.

2. Have students form groups of 3 or 4 (as required by the Role Play script). Distribute the activity sheets. Tell the students that they will be reading the script, identifying the speakers, choosing characters, and acting out the Role Play.

3. Review the directions and check for comprehension by asking: *Do you complete the activity by yourself?* [no] *Do you say the lines out loud?* [yes]

4. Focus attention on the script and the first two lines. Read them out loud and have students identify the speakers of each line. Have students write the character's name by the second line.

5. Set a time limit (15–20 minutes) for the groups to read the script and decide which character is speaking each line. Have students write the

characters' names on the space provided. Call time and ask student volunteers to read each line and identify the speaker.

6. Have students in groups add more lines to the script and replace words for the underlined parts of the script. Tell students they can use the *Dictionary* to check their spelling. Ask groups to call out new or changed lines and write them on the board.

7. Have students act out the Role Play in their groups. Monitor student practice by walking around to help with pronunciation problems such as register, stress, and intonation. Encourage students to use appropriate movement and gestures.

8. Have groups act out their Role Plays for the class. Encourage the class to applaud after each performance.

9. Do the **What's Next?** activity with the class.

Hot Tip *If you have access to a video camera, record the performances and play them back for the students to enjoy and evaluate.*

For Multilevel Classes

Low-Beginning: This activity is not recommended for this group.

High-Beginning: Have these students complete the activity as outlined above.

Low-Intermediate: Have these students add lines for a new character of their choosing.

Activity Objective: Student pairs analyze statements and decide which of two positions a statement supports. Students write sentences about their opinions.

Before Class: Duplicate the selected Take a Stand activity sheet for each student. Look over the activity sheet to determine vocabulary students may need to review.

Quick Start

Ready: Write the activity title on the board and discuss it as a class. Read a sample statement. Survey the class by asking which position they think the statement supports. Ask student volunteers to discuss their answers. Review vocabulary students may need for the activity.	**Set:** Distribute the activity sheets and review the directions. Read and check the first statement as a class and discuss it.	**Go:** Have students complete the activity sheet independently, then have students form pairs. Partners compare answers, discuss, and write sentences about their opinions based on the discussion.

Step by Step

1. Write the activity title on the board and discuss it as a class. Ask related questions to get students thinking about the topic. For example, for a discussion on preferring cats or dogs, ask: *Do you have a dog or cat? Why do you like your dog or cat?*

2. Read a sample statement. Survey the class by asking which position they think the statement supports. Ask student volunteers to discuss their answer. Challenge students to think of vocabulary that relates to both positions. Allow time for brainstorming and write these words on the board.

3. Tell students they will read statements and decide which position each supports.

4. Distribute the activity sheets and review the directions. Check for comprehension by asking: *Do you check both columns?* [no] *Do you compare opinions with a partner?* [yes] *Can you use your Dictionary to check your vocabulary?* [yes]

5. Read the first statement as a class and have students decide which column they should check.

6. Set a time limit (10–15 minutes) for students to work on their own, reading the statements and checking the appropriate columns. Have students write two more statements for the chart. Ask student volunteers to write their statements on the board and have them tell you which position they support.

7. Have students form pairs and compare their activity sheets. Ask students to write their ideas and their partners' ideas about the topic by completing the two sentences below the chart. Monitor student progress by walking around to help students' conversations and writing.

8. Do the **What's Next** activity as a class.

Hot Tip *Make sure students have ample time to practice new vocabulary in context before doing the activity.*

For Multilevel Classes

Low-Beginning: This activity is not recommended for this group.

High-Beginning: Have these students complete the activity as outlined above.

Low-Intermediate: Complete the activity sheets and then have these students participate in a debate in which each side will present their position to the class.

Technology Words

1. Work with a partner. Cut apart the cards.
2. Write the Word List words on the back of the cards.
3. Student A: Show the picture to your partner.
   Student B: Say the word or phrase.
4. Take turns.

WORD LIST

1.1	LCD projector	1.5	cash register	1.9	answering machine	1.13	phone jack
1.2	computer	1.6	smart phone	1.10	text message	1.14	headset
1.3	overhead projector	1.7	pay phone	1.11	calling card	1.15	antenna
1.4	calculator	1.8	cordless phone	1.12	access number	1.16	cord

Everyday Language

Information Needed

1. Work with a partner. Cut apart the cards.
2. Write the Word List words on the back of the cards.
3. Student A: Show the picture to your partner.
   Student B: Say the word or phrase.
4. Take turns.

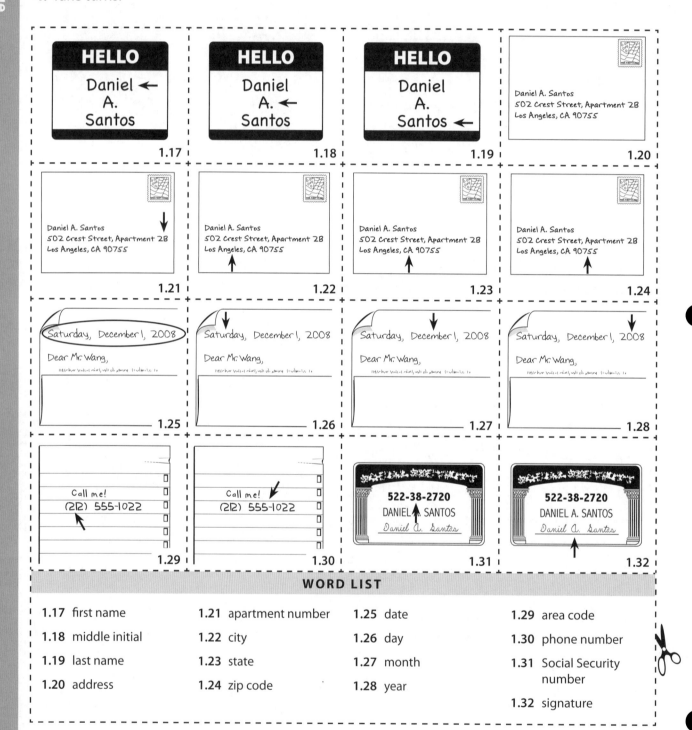

WORD LIST			
1.17 first name	1.21 apartment number	1.25 date	1.29 area code
1.18 middle initial	1.22 city	1.26 day	1.30 phone number
1.19 last name	1.23 state	1.27 month	1.31 Social Security number
1.20 address	1.24 zip code	1.28 year	1.32 signature

Everyday Language

Reasons to Be Happy

1. Work with 3 classmates. Cut apart the cards. Put them face down in a pile.
2. Student A: Pick a card. Describe the word or phrase on the card.
   Students B, C, and D: Guess the word or phrase.
3. The first student to guess correctly keeps the card.
4. Take turns.

WORD LIST

1.33 pass a test	**1.37** birthday	**1.41** Thanksgiving	**1.45** use a gift card
1.34 make progress	**1.38** wedding	**1.42** Christmas	**1.46** buy
1.35 get good grades	**1.39** anniversary	**1.43** pay back money	**1.47** sale price
1.36 accept an invitation	**1.40** vacation	**1.44** get change	**1.48** hug

Everyday Language

What Students Do

1. Work with 3 classmates. Cut apart the cards. Put the cards face down in a pile.
2. Student A: Pick a card. Silently act out the action.
   Student B: Ask *What is he / she doing?*
   Students C and D: Answer the question using the present continuous. (*He is sitting down.*)
   Student B: Write what your classmates say.
3. Take turns.

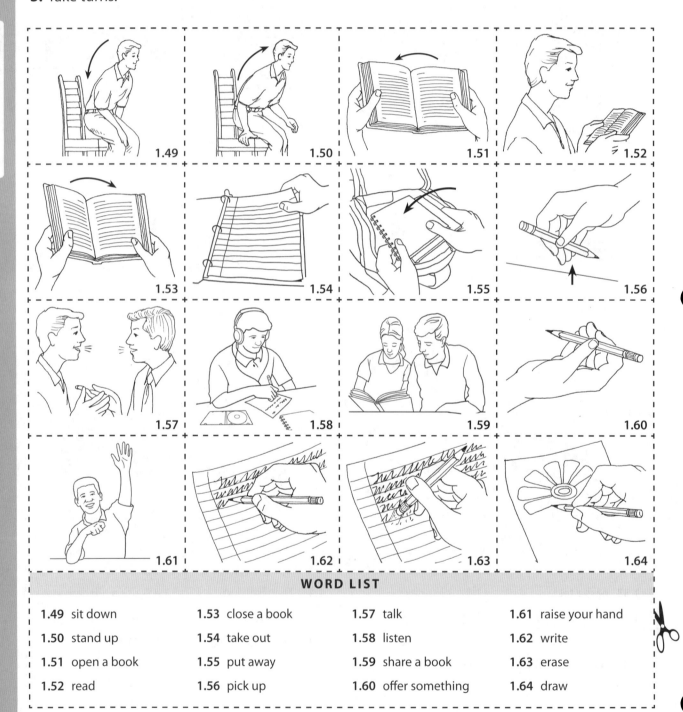

WORD LIST			
1.49 sit down	**1.53** close a book	**1.57** talk	**1.61** raise your hand
1.50 stand up	**1.54** take out	**1.58** listen	**1.62** write
1.51 open a book	**1.55** put away	**1.59** share a book	**1.63** erase
1.52 read	**1.56** pick up	**1.60** offer something	**1.64** draw

How's the weather? Grid

1. Use this grid with the picture cards on page 8.
2. Student A: Put one picture on each square on the grid. Don't show your partner your grid.
    Use the picture and the square to tell your partner a sentence.
    (*It's going to be sunny today.*)
   Student B: Listen to your partner. Check what you heard.
    (*Did you say it's going to be sunny today?*)
    Put the picture on the correct square on the grid.
3. When the grids are full, compare them. If they are the same, change roles. If not, try again.

today	tomorrow	this week	next week
this month	next month	in February	in April
in July	in October	on Monday	on Tuesday
on Wednesday	on Thursday	on Friday	this weekend

Everyday Language

GRAMMAR ACTIVITY

How's the weather? Cards

1. Use these picture cards with the grid on page 7.
2. Work with a partner. Cut apart the cards.

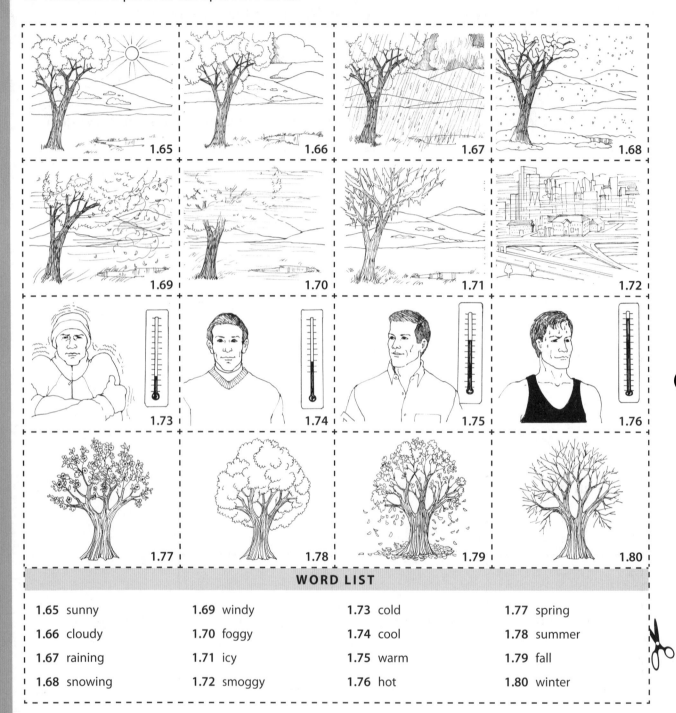

WORD LIST

1.65 sunny	**1.69** windy	**1.73** cold	**1.77** spring
1.66 cloudy	**1.70** foggy	**1.74** cool	**1.78** summer
1.67 raining	**1.71** icy	**1.75** warm	**1.79** fall
1.68 snowing	**1.72** smoggy	**1.76** hot	**1.80** winter

Everyday Language

Where's the pencil?

1. Work with 2 classmates.
2. Label what you see in the picture. Take turns.
3. Check your spelling in the *OPD*.

student

▶ **What's Next?** Your teacher will describe things on a desk and inside the drawers. Listen to your teacher and draw what she says. When you are finished, compare your picture with a classmate's. Are the pictures the same?

What's in the office? A

1. Find a partner with page 11 (B). Don't show your partner this paper.
2. Describe Picture A to your partner. Your partner will draw what you say.
3. Answer your partner's questions.

4. Listen to your partner describe Picture B. Draw what you hear. You can ask questions like these: *Did you say on the ____ or under the ____? Where are they? How many are there?*
5. When both pictures are complete, compare them.

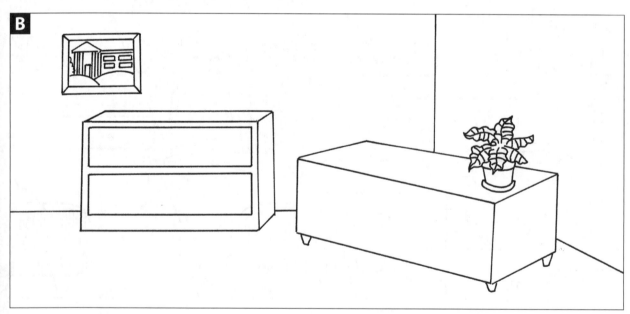

▶ **What's Next?** Describe a room in the school to your teacher. Your teacher will draw what you say. Ask the teacher to guess which room it is.

What's in the office? B

1. Find a partner with page 10 (A). Don't show your partner this paper.
2. Listen to your partner describe Picture A. Draw what you hear. You can ask questions like these: *Did you say on the ____ or under the ____? Where are they? How many are there?*

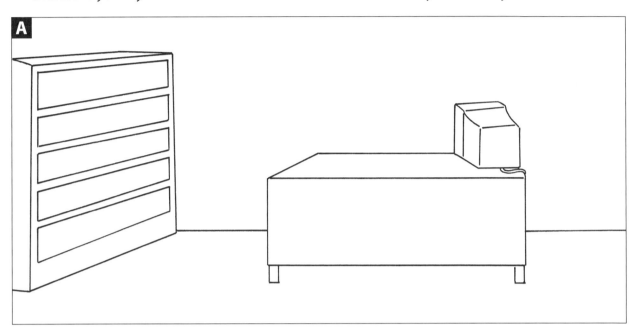

3. Describe Picture B to your partner. Your partner will draw what you say.
4. Answer your partner's questions.
5. When both pictures are complete, compare them.

▶ **What's Next?** Describe a room in the school to your teacher. Your teacher will draw what you say. Ask the teacher to guess which room it is.

Everyday Language

B

What is that?

1. Work with 3 or 4 classmates. Choose a Recorder.

2. Use the cards to make 10 different sentences or questions. The Recorder writes them down.

THIS	THAT	IS	ISN'T
A	AN	HERE	EXPENSIVE
THICK	SOFT	BEAUTIFUL	BIG
BLACK	BLUE	SWEATER	DICTIONARY
COMPUTER	CHAIR	.	?

▶ **What's Next?** Share your sentences with the class. Which group made the most sentences? the most questions?

School Days A

1. Find a partner with page 14 (B). Look at each other's picture.
2. Find 10 differences with your partner. Write the differences in the chart.

	A	B
1.	The first runner is wearing white.	The first runner is wearing black.
2.		
3.		
4.		
5.		
6.		
7.		
8.		
9.		
10.		

▶ **What's Next?** Work with a partner. Compare your school to the ones in the pictures. How are they different? How are they similar?

Everyday Language

A

School Days B

1. Find a partner with page 13 (A). Look at each other's picture.
2. Find 10 differences with your partner. Write the differences in the chart.

	A	**B**
1.	The first runner is wearing white.	The first runner is wearing black.
2.		
3.		
4.		
5.		
6.		
7.		
8.		
9.		
10.		

▶ **What's Next?** Work with a partner. Compare your school to the ones in the pictures. How are they different? How are they similar?

Everyday Language

B

Going Shopping

1. Read the questions. Mark your answers with a ✔.
2. Survey 5 classmates. Write their names, and mark their answer with a ✔.

Would you rather …	My answers	_____ answers	_____ answers	_____ answers	_____ answers	_____ answers
use a credit card **OR** use a debit card?						
pay regular price **OR** pay sale price?						
pay cash **OR** write a check?						
buy expensive things **OR** buy cheap things?						
pay with coins **OR** pay with bills?						
write a personal check **OR** use a traveler's check?						

3. Write sentences about each classmate you surveyed.

   Juanita would rather use a credit card than a debit card.

   1. _____

   2. _____

   3. _____

   4. _____

   5. _____

4. Work with 2 classmates. Read your sentences out loud and compare them.

▶ **What's Next?** Write sentences about your answers.

Everyday Language

GRAMMAR ACTIVITY

Everyday Language

The Birthday Party

1. Work with 2 classmates.
2. Look at the picture. Read the first sentence. Think of more sentences to write about the picture.
3. Take turns writing sentences to continue the story.
4. Check your spelling in the *OPD*.

It's Mikhail's birthday, and his friends are having a party for him.

_____

_____

_____

_____

_____

_____

_____

_____

_____

▶ **What's Next?** Your friend is having a birthday party. Tell your classmates who the friend is and describe the size, color, and price of the gift(s) you are bringing.

What's that number? A

1. Find a partner with page 18 (B). Don't show your partner this paper.
2. Look at A. Ask your partner about the missing information in this phone bill. You can ask questions like these: *When did Eliza call _____? What day did Eliza call _____? How long was the call to _____?*
3. Write the missing information.

A

JBB Telephone Company

	Eliza Oxford 1234 Elm Avenue Pelham, NY	Account Number (914) 555-9678	Statement Date April 14	STATEMENT

CALL SUMMARY

LOCAL	Date	Time	Place and Number Called	Rate	Minutes
	Mar 15	9:15 PM	Pelham, NY _____	Night	____

DOMESTIC	Date	Time	Place and Number Called	Rate	Minutes
	Mar 13	_____	Fairfield NJ (973) 555-6896	_____	2
	_____	9:30 PM	Scottsdale, AZ _____	Night	____
	Mar 27	_____	Encino, CA (818) 555-7803	_____	10

INTERNATIONAL	Date	Time	Place and Number Called	Rate	Minutes
	Mar 17	8:19 AM	Seoul, Korea _____	Day	____
	_____	2:00 PM	Warsaw, Poland (48) 22-555-7863	_____	6

4. Look at B. Use this phone bill to answer your partner's questions.
5. When you are finished, compare your phone bills with your partner's.

B

STATEMENT DATE
April 14

PATRICK DOMINGO
5231 Oak Drive
Encino, CA

ACCOUNT NUMBER
(818) 555-7803

VBL Telephone Calls

CALL SUMMARY

	Date	Time	Place	Number Called	Rate	Minutes
LOCAL	Mar 13	10:23 AM	Encino, CA	(818) 555-7115	Day	8
DOMESTIC	Mar 14	6:10 AM	Pelham, NY	(914) 555-9678	Day	5
	Mar 15	3:30 PM	Seattle, WA	(206) 555-7145	Day	22
	Mar 31	8:15 PM	Boulder, CO	(303) 555-7000	Day	3
INTERNATIONAL	Mar 12	8:19 AM	London, GB	(44) 171-555-7000	Day	4
	Mar 28	11:00 PM	Madrid, Spain	(34) 1-555-8204	Night	9

▶ **What's Next?** Look at the time zone map on page 19 of the *OPD*. What time was it in each city when Eliza and Patrick made their calls? Who do you think they were calling? What did they say? Write a short conversation using greetings and everyday conversation.

What's that number? B

1. Find a partner with page 17 (A). Don't show your partner this paper.

2. Look at A. Use this phone bill to answer your partner's questions.

A

JBB Telephone Company		Eliza Oxford 1234 Elm Avenue Pelham, NY	Account Number (914) 555-9678	Statement Date April 14		STATEMENT	

CALL SUMMARY

LOCAL	Date	Time	Place and Number Called		Rate	Minutes
	Mar 15	9:15 PM	Pelham, NY	(914) 555-3210	Night	23
DOMESTIC	Date	Time	Place and Number Called		Rate	Minutes
	Mar 13	5:10 PM	Fairfield, NJ	(973) 555-6896	Day	2
	Mar 19	9:30 PM	Scottsdale, AZ	(602) 555-7145	Night	6
	Mar 27	10:57 AM	Encino, CA	(818) 555-7803	Day	10
INTERNATIONAL	Date	Time	Place and Number Called		Rate	Minutes
	Mar 17	8:19 AM	Seoul, Korea	(82) 44-555-3446	Day	2
	Mar 25	2:00 PM	Warsaw, Poland	(48) 22-555-7863	Day	6

3. Look at B. Ask your partner about the missing information in this phone bill. You can ask questions like these: *When did Patrick call _____? What day did Patrick call _____? How long was the call to _____?*

4. Write the missing information.

5. When you are finished, compare your phone bills with your partner's.

B

STATEMENT DATE	
April 14	

PATRICK DOMINGO
5231 Oak Drive
Encino, CA

ACCOUNT NUMBER
(818) 555-7803

VBL *Telephone Calls*

CALL SUMMARY

	Date	Time	Place	Number Called	Rate	Minutes
LOCAL	Mar 13	10:23 AM	Encino, CA	(818) 555-7115	_____	8
DOMESTIC	Mar 14	_____	Pelham, NY	(914) 555-9678	Day	5
	_____	3:30 PM	Seattle, WA	_____	_____	22
	Mar 31	_____	Boulder, CO	(303) 555-7000	_____	___
INTERNATIONAL	_____	8:19 AM	London, GB	(44) 171-555-7000	_____	___
	Mar 28	_____	Madrid, Spain	_____	Night	9

▶ **What's Next?** Look at the time zone map on page 19 of the *OPD*. What time was it in each city when Eliza and Patrick made their calls? Who do you think they were calling? What did they say? Write a short conversation using greetings and everyday conversation.

The Best Sweater

1. Work with 3 classmates.
2. Write the character next to each line.
3. Choose your character. Write other lines you could say.
4. Practice saying the lines. Act out the role play.

The Scene

salesclerk in a busy store trying to help three customers

The Characters

Salesclerk
Customer A (exchanging)
Customer B (returning)
Customer C (buying)

The Props

different colored sweaters and/or other clothing items

The Script

Salesclerk:	May I help you?
_____	I'd like to return this <u>sweater</u>.*
_____	Excuse me, I was here first.
_____	I'll help you after I help this customer.
_____	I want to return this sweater because it's too <u>big</u>.
_____	Excuse me, can I exchange this for <u>a green sweater</u>?
_____	Sure, we have some great <u>red</u> and <u>green sweaters</u> on sale over there.
_____	Oh, really? I'll take a look.
_____	How much are those <u>thick sweaters</u>?
_____	They are $<u>15.99</u>, and they are on sale.
_____	That's cheap! Can I pay by <u>check</u>?

*You can use other vocabulary for the underlined words.

▶ **What's Next?** Work with a partner. Plan a sale of items you don't want anymore. Make a list of the items and their prices. What would you buy with the money from the sale?

Everyday Language

Everyday Language

Learn at School or at Home?

1. Think about reasons to learn at a school or learn at home.
2. Read the statements in the chart.
3. Write 2 more statements in the chart.
4. If the statement shows that learning at a school is a good idea, ✔ that column. If the statement shows that learning at home is a good idea, ✔ that column.

Statements	learning at a school	learning at home
You can discuss a problem with a classmate.		
You can study at any time of the night or day.		
There are programs on TV that teach school subjects.		
You can use the gym, library, and computer lab.		
You can work with a counselor.		
You can buy textbooks and CDs to use at home.		
You can talk to teachers.		
Some classes at school have too many students.		
You can keep your books in a locker.		
You don't have to eat lunch in the cafeteria.		

5. Work with a partner. Compare your ideas.
6. Write your and your partner's ideas.

I think that learning at _____ is a good idea because _____

_____

My partner thinks that learning at _____ is a good idea because

_____

▶ **What's Next?** Work as a class. How many students think learning at a school is a good idea? How many students think learning at home is good idea? Draw a bar graph on the board. Then discuss the results.

Describing People

1. Work with a partner. Cut apart the cards.

2. Write the Word List words on the back of the cards.

3. Student A: Show the picture to your partner.
   Student B: Say the word or phrase.

4. Take turns.

WORD LIST			
2.1 infant	**2.5** girl	**2.9** senior citizen	**2.13** tall
2.2 baby	**2.6** teenager	**2.10** young	**2.14** short
2.3 toddler	**2.7** man	**2.11** middle-aged	**2.15** thin
2.4 boy	**2.8** woman	**2.12** elderly	**2.16** heavy

Life Events

1. Work with a partner. Cut apart the cards.
2. Write the Word List words on the back of the cards.
3. Student A: Show the picture to your partner.
   Student B: Say the word or phrase.
4. Take turns.

WORD LIST

2.17 be born	**2.21** learn to drive	**2.25** fall in love	**2.29** buy a home
2.18 start school	**2.22** get a job	**2.26** get engaged	**2.30** become a grandparent
2.19 immigrate	**2.23** become a citizen	**2.27** get married	
2.20 graduate	**2.24** go to college	**2.28** have a baby	**2.31** retire
			2.32 die

People

People

Families and Parenting

1. Work with 3 classmates. Cut apart the cards. Put them face down in a pile.

2. Student A: Pick a card. Describe the word or phrase on the card.
　　Students B, C, and D: Guess the word or phrase.

3. The first student to guess correctly keeps the card.

4. Take turns.

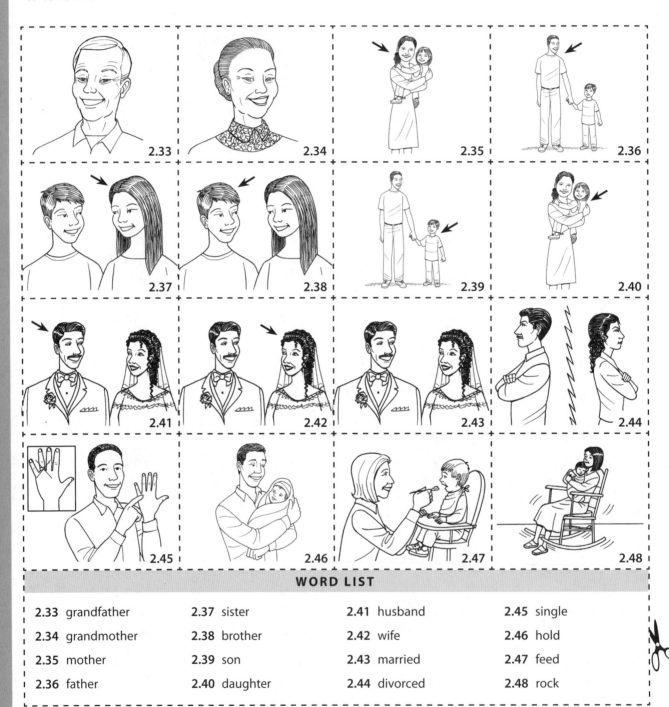

WORD LIST

2.33 grandfather	**2.37** sister	**2.41** husband	**2.45** single
2.34 grandmother	**2.38** brother	**2.42** wife	**2.46** hold
2.35 mother	**2.39** son	**2.43** married	**2.47** feed
2.36 father	**2.40** daughter	**2.44** divorced	**2.48** rock

Daily Routines

1. Work with 3 classmates. Cut apart the cards. Put the cards face down in a pile.
2. Student A: Pick a card. Silently act out the action.
   Student B: Ask *What did he / she do?*
   Students C and D: Answer the question using the past tense. (*She woke up.*)
   Student B: Write what your classmates say.
3. Take turns.

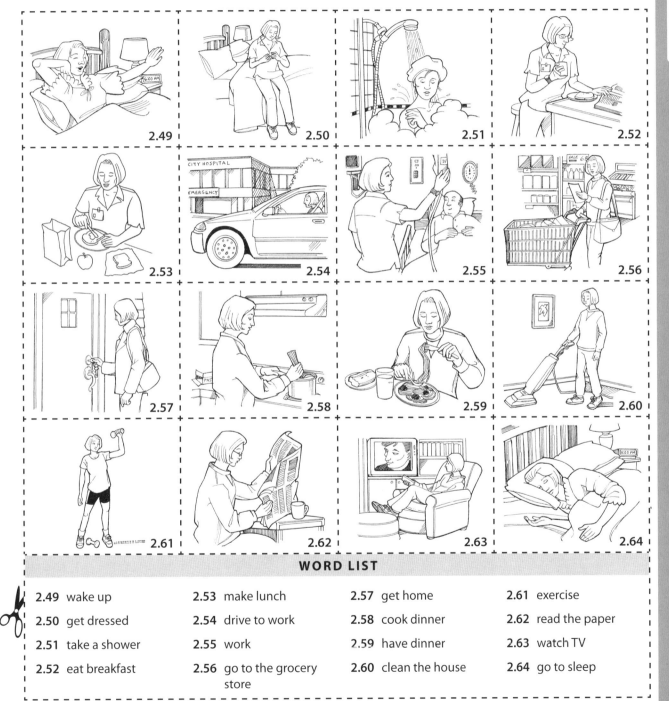

WORD LIST

2.49 wake up	**2.53** make lunch	**2.57** get home	**2.61** exercise
2.50 get dressed	**2.54** drive to work	**2.58** cook dinner	**2.62** read the paper
2.51 take a shower	**2.55** work	**2.59** have dinner	**2.63** watch TV
2.52 eat breakfast	**2.56** go to the grocery store	**2.60** clean the house	**2.64** go to sleep

People

GRAMMAR ACTIVITY

How's your family? Grid

1. Use this grid with the picture cards on page 27.

2. Student A: Put one picture on each square on the grid. Don't show your partner your grid.
Use the picture and the square to tell your partner a sentence.
(*Frank's uncle is happy.*)

Student B: Listen to your partner. Check what you heard.
(*Did you say Frank's uncle is happy?*)
Put the picture on the correct square on the grid.

3. When the grids are full, compare them. If they are the same, change roles. If not, try again.

Frank's uncle	Ellen's mother	his wife	Kelly's aunt
Ms. Lee's son	Rosa's cousin	Chen's daughter	Harry's sister
Mr. Garcia's grandmother	Susan's stepmother	Bill's nephew	Joy's niece
Lin's father	her husband	Mr. Price's wife	their cousin

How's your family? Cards

1. Use these picture cards with the grid on page 26.

2. Work with a partner. Cut apart the cards.

WORD LIST

2.65 happy	**2.69** excited	**2.73** comfortable	**2.77** cold
2.66 scared	**2.70** lonely	**2.74** uncomfortable	**2.78** sad
2.67 nervous	**2.71** tired	**2.75** sick	**2.79** sleepy
2.68 thirsty	**2.72** bored	**2.76** hungry	**2.80** embarrassed

People

Grandma's Party

1. Work with 2 classmates.
2. Label what you see in the picture. Take turns.
3. Check your spelling in the *OPD*.

▶ **What's Next?** Work with a partner. Draw a picture of a child, teenager, or adult that you know. (You can use a photograph to help you.) Write a description of the person and read it to your partner.

Caring for the Baby A

1. Find a partner with page 30 (B). Don't show your partner this paper.
2. Describe Picture A to your partner. Your partner will draw what you say.
3. Answer your partner's questions.

4. Listen to your partner describe Picture B. Draw what you hear. You can ask questions like these: *What's on the table? What's next to the _____?*
5. When both pictures are complete, compare them.

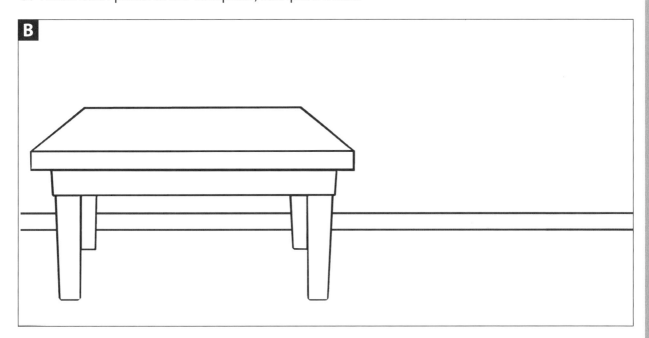

▶ **What's Next?** Continue working with your partner. Look at page 37 of the *OPD*. Write sentences about two more items to put in each picture. What are the items? Where do they go?

Caring for the Baby B

1. Find a partner with page 29 (A). Don't show your partner this paper.
2. Listen to your partner describe Picture A. Draw what you hear. You can ask questions like these: *What's on the shelf? What's next to the _____?*

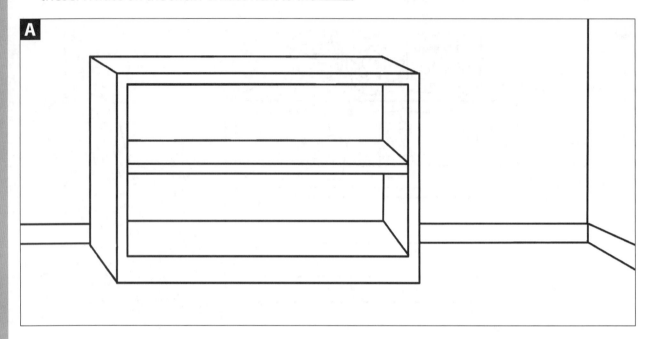

3. Describe Picture B to your partner. Your partner will draw what you say.
4. Answer your partner's questions.
5. When both pictures are complete, compare them.

▶ **What's Next?** Continue working with your partner. Look at page 37 of the *OPD*. Write sentences about two more items to put in each picture. What are the items? Where do they go?

How do they feel?

1. Work with 3 or 4 classmates. Choose a Recorder.
2. Use the cards to make 10 different sentences or questions. The Recorder writes them down.

YOU	YOUR	BROTHER	SISTER
CHILD	IS	NOT	ARE
AND	COMFORTABLE	NERVOUS	SICK
HOT	THIRSTY	SLEEPY	LONELY
COLD	HUNGRY	.	?

▶ **What's Next?** Share your sentences with the class. Which group made the most sentences? the most questions?

People

GRAMMAR ACTIVITY

People

What a day! A

1. Find a partner with page 33 (B). Look at each other's picture.

2. Find 10 differences with your partner. Write the differences in the chart.

	A	**B**
1.	The son is getting up.	The son is sleeping.
2.		
3.		
4.		
5.		
6.		
7.		
8.		
9.		
10.		

▶ **What's Next?** Work with a partner. Talk about your daily routine. What's the same? What's different?

What a day! B

1. Find a partner with page 32 (A). Look at each other's picture.
2. Find 10 differences with your partner. Write the differences in the chart.

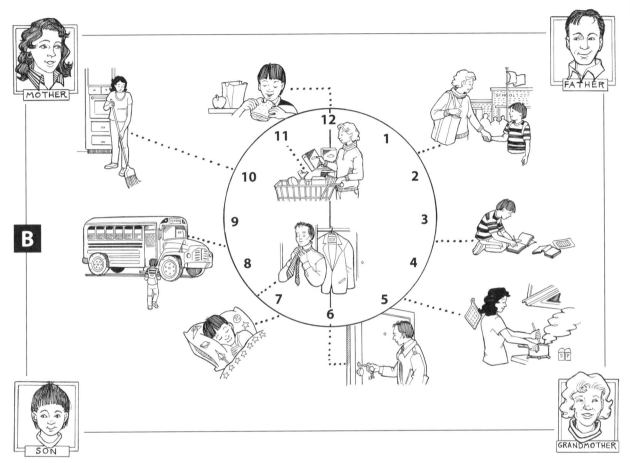

	A		B
1.	The son is getting up.		The son is sleeping.
2.			
3.			
4.			
5.			
6.			
7.			
8.			
9.			
10.			

▶ **What's Next?** Work with a partner. Talk about your daily routine. What's the same? What's different?

People

GRAMMAR ACTIVITY

What do you do every day?

1. Read the questions. Mark your answers with a ✔.

2. Survey 5 classmates. Write their names, and mark their answer with a ✔.

Do you …	My answers	_____ answers	_____ answers	_____ answers	_____ answers	_____ answers
get up on time every day **OR** get up late every day?						
take the bus to school every day **OR** drive to school every day?						
cook dinner every night **OR** cook dinner on some nights?						
watch TV every night **OR** watch TV on some nights?						
go to bed early every night **OR** go to bed late every night?						

3. Write sentences about each classmate you surveyed.

Miguel gets up on time every day.

1. _____

2. _____

3. _____

4. _____

5. _____

4. Work with 2 classmates. Read your sentences out loud and compare them.

► **What's Next?** Write sentences about your answers.

Happy Times

1. Work with 2 classmates.
2. Look at the pictures. Read the first sentence. Think of more sentences to write about the pictures.
3. Take turns writing sentences to continue the story.
4. Check your spelling in the *OPD*.

_____ Joanne and Frank got married in 1996. _____

_____

_____

_____

_____

_____

_____

_____

_____

_____

▶ **What's Next?** Work with a partner. Think about a happy time in your life. What happened? Write sentences. Then tell your partner about the happy time.

Family Trees A

1. Find a partner with page 37 (B). Don't show your partner this paper.

2. Look at A. Ask your partner about the missing names in this family tree. You can ask questions like these: *Who is Elena's husband? What's the name of Andy's cousin?*

3. Write the missing names.

A

4. Look at B. Use this family tree to answer your partner's questions.

5. When you are finished, compare your family trees with your partner's.

B

▶ **What's Next?** Draw a family tree for a part of your family or a family you know. Share the family tree with the class.

36   Unit Two

Family Trees B

1. Find a partner with page 36 (A). Don't show your partner this paper.
2. Look at A. Use this family tree to answer your partner's questions.

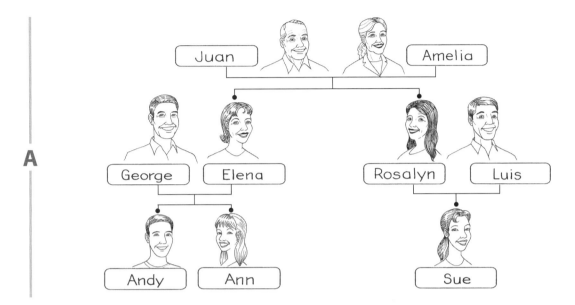

3. Look at B. Ask your partner about the missing names in this family tree. You can ask questions like these: *What's the name of John's wife? Does Mindy have an aunt? What's her name?*
4. Write the missing names.
5. When you are finished, compare your family trees with your partner's.

► **What's Next?** Draw a family tree for a part of your family or a family you know. Share the family tree with the class.

People

Please don't cut it too short!

1. Work with 3 classmates.
2. Write the character next to each line.
3. Choose your character. Write other lines you could say.
4. Practice saying the lines. Act out the role play.

The Scene
a small hair salon for men and women

The Characters
Receptionist
Customer A
Customer B
Hair stylist

The Props
an appointment book
one or two mirrors
a comb and a brush

The Script

Receptionist: Hi, what time is your appointment?

_____   It's at 4:30.*

_____   Mine is at 5:30.

_____   OK. Could you both wait here? Your stylist will be here soon.

_____   Hi, you're perming your hair today, right?

_____   No, I want to cut my hair, actually.

_____   We can do that. How short do you want it?

_____   Please don't cut it too short!

_____   Thanks for waiting. What do you want to do today?

_____   Well, I need a new hairstyle.

_____   How about perming and coloring your hair?

_____   _____

_____   _____

_____   _____

*You can use other vocabulary for the underlined words.

▶ **What's Next?** Work with a partner. Talk about the hairstyles of famous singers or movie stars you like.

Large or Small Families?

1. Think about reasons to have large or small families.
2. Read the statements in the chart.
3. Write 2 more statements in the chart.
4. If the statement shows that having large families is a good idea, ✔ that column. If the statement shows that having small families is a good idea, ✔ that column.

Statements	having large families	having small families
Parents will have more money to spend on their children.		
Younger children can use older children's toys.		
Food, clothing, and medicine are expensive for a family.		
Older children can teach things to younger children.		
Older children can look after younger children.		
Grandparents like having many grandchildren.		
Children will have many brothers and sisters to play with.		
Children can help each other when parents are old.		
Children may have to share bedrooms.		
Large families may need more than one car.		

5. Work with a partner. Compare your ideas.
6. Write your and your partner's ideas.

I think that having _____ families is a good idea because _____

_____

My partner thinks that having _____ families is a good idea because

_____

▶ **What's Next?** Work as a class. How many students prefer large families? small families? Draw a bar graph on the board. Then discuss the results.

Let's fix it!

1. Work with a partner. Cut apart the cards.
2. Write the Word List words on the back of the cards.
3. Student A: Show the picture to your partner.
   Student B: Say the word or phrase.
4. Take turns.

WORD LIST

3.1 roofer	3.5 repair person	3.9 carpenter	3.13 exterminator
3.2 leaking roof	3.6 broken window	3.10 broken step	3.14 mouse
3.3 electrician	3.7 locksmith	3.11 plumber	3.15 ants
3.4 power is out	3.8 broken lock	3.12 dripping faucet	3.16 termites

Around the House

1. Work with a partner. Cut apart the cards.

2. Write the Word List words on the back of the cards.

3. Student A: Show the picture to your partner.
Student B: Say the word or phrase.

4. Take turns.

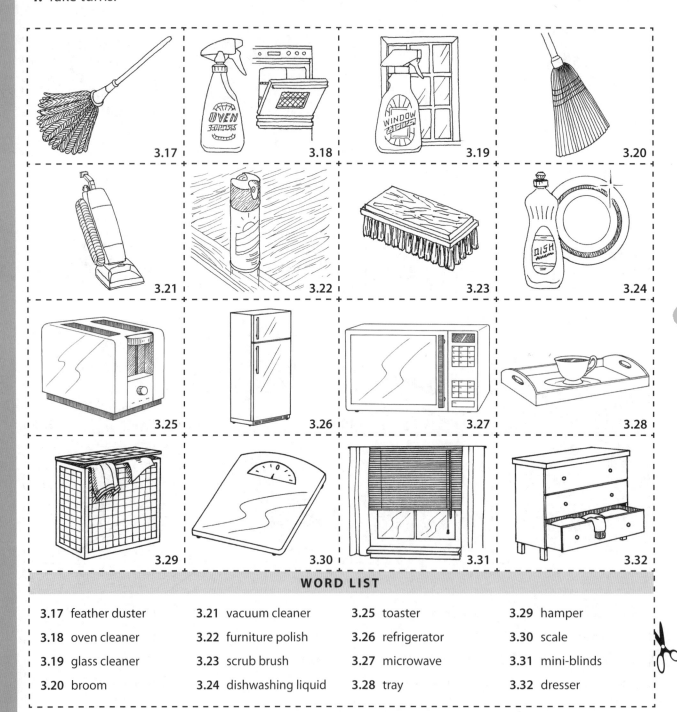

WORD LIST

3.17 feather duster	3.21 vacuum cleaner	3.25 toaster	3.29 hamper
3.18 oven cleaner	3.22 furniture polish	3.26 refrigerator	3.30 scale
3.19 glass cleaner	3.23 scrub brush	3.27 microwave	3.31 mini-blinds
3.20 broom	3.24 dishwashing liquid	3.28 tray	3.32 dresser

▶ **Guess What? Cards** (See page xiv for Teacher's Notes.) OPD pages 53, 59

Housing

Outside and Inside

1. Work with 3 classmates. Cut apart the cards. Put them face down in a pile.
2. Student A: Pick a card. Describe the word or phrase on the card.
   Students B, C, and D: Guess the word or phrase.
3. The first student to guess correctly keeps the card.
4. Take turns.

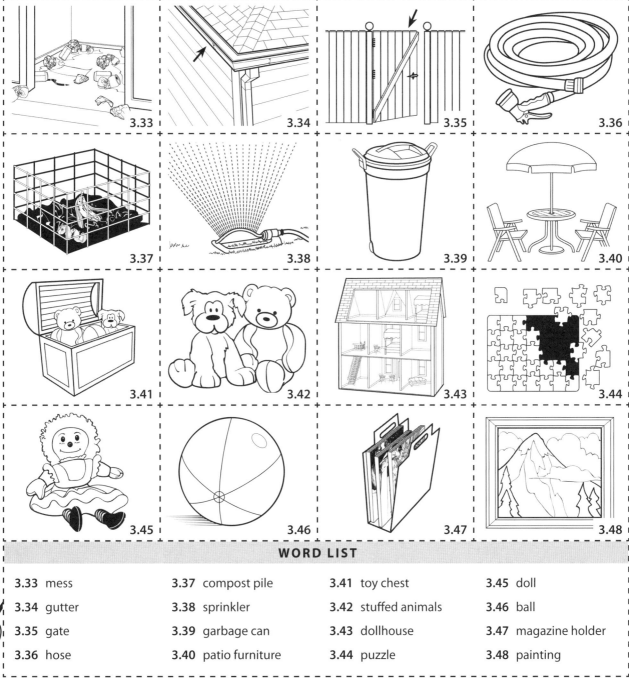

3.33
3.34
3.35
3.36
3.37
3.38
3.39
3.40
3.41
3.42
3.43
3.44
3.45
3.46
3.47
3.48

WORD LIST

3.33 mess	3.37 compost pile	3.41 toy chest	3.45 doll
3.34 gutter	3.38 sprinkler	3.42 stuffed animals	3.46 ball
3.35 gate	3.39 garbage can	3.43 dollhouse	3.47 magazine holder
3.36 hose	3.40 patio furniture	3.44 puzzle	3.48 painting

So Much Work, Not Enough Time!

1. Work with 3 classmates. Cut apart the cards. Put the cards face down in a pile.

2. Student A: Pick a card. Silently act out the action.

   Student B: Ask *What is he / she going to do?*

   Students C and D: Answer the question using the future tense. (*She is going to garden.*)

   Student B: Write what your classmates say.

3. Take turns.

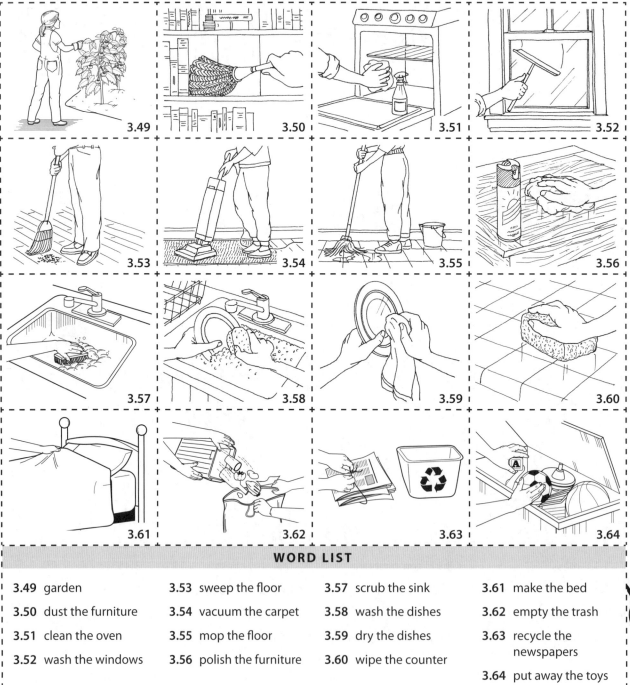

WORD LIST	

3.49 garden	**3.53** sweep the floor	**3.57** scrub the sink	**3.61** make the bed
3.50 dust the furniture	**3.54** vacuum the carpet	**3.58** wash the dishes	**3.62** empty the trash
3.51 clean the oven	**3.55** mop the floor	**3.59** dry the dishes	**3.63** recycle the newspapers
3.52 wash the windows	**3.56** polish the furniture	**3.60** wipe the counter	**3.64** put away the toys

(Side tab: Housing / GRAMMAR ACTIVITY)

Where is it? Grid

1. Use this grid with the picture cards on page 46.
2. Student A: Put one picture on each square on the grid. Don't show your partner your grid.
   Use the picture and the square to tell your partner a sentence.
   (*The entertainment center is next to the window.*)
   Student B: Listen to your partner. Check what you heard.
   (*Did you say the entertainment center is next to the window?*)
   Put the picture on the correct square on the grid.
3. When the grids are full, compare them. If they are the same, change roles. If not, try again.

next to the window	under the painting	by the door	in the middle of the room
on the right side of the room	on the left side of the room	under the window	on the entertainment center
in front of the wall	in the cabinet	between the houseplant and the floor lamp	next to the chair
near the rug	on the mantle	on the coffee table	on the end table

Housing

GRAMMAR ACTIVITY

Housing

GRAMMAR ACTIVITY

Where is it? Cards

1. Use these picture cards with the grid on page 45.

2. Work with a partner. Cut apart the cards.

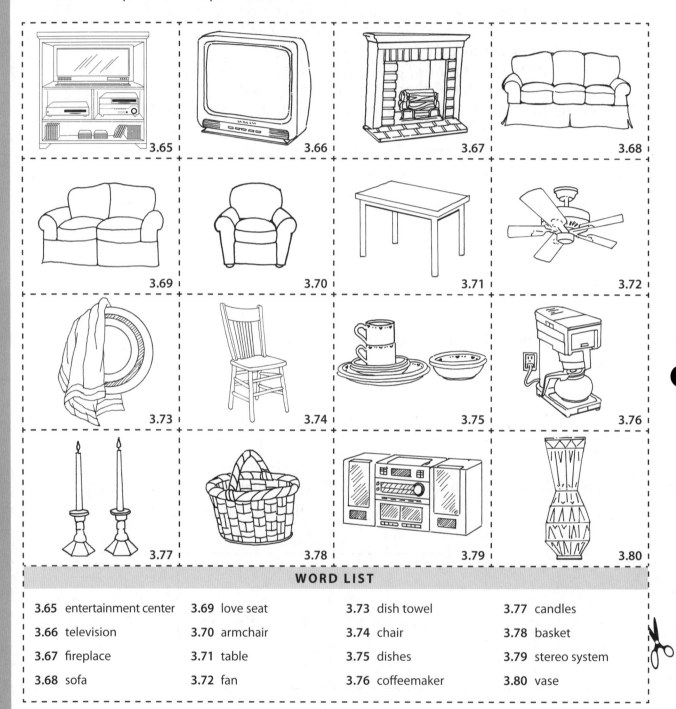

WORD LIST	

3.65 entertainment center **3.69** love seat **3.73** dish towel **3.77** candles

3.66 television **3.70** armchair **3.74** chair **3.78** basket

3.67 fireplace **3.71** table **3.75** dishes **3.79** stereo system

3.68 sofa **3.72** fan **3.76** coffeemaker **3.80** vase

▶ **Round Table Label** (See page xvii for Teacher's Notes.)

OPD pages 55–56, 58–59

Housing

A Yard Sale

1. Work with 2 classmates.
2. Label what you see in the picture. Take turns.
3. Check your spelling in the *OPD*.

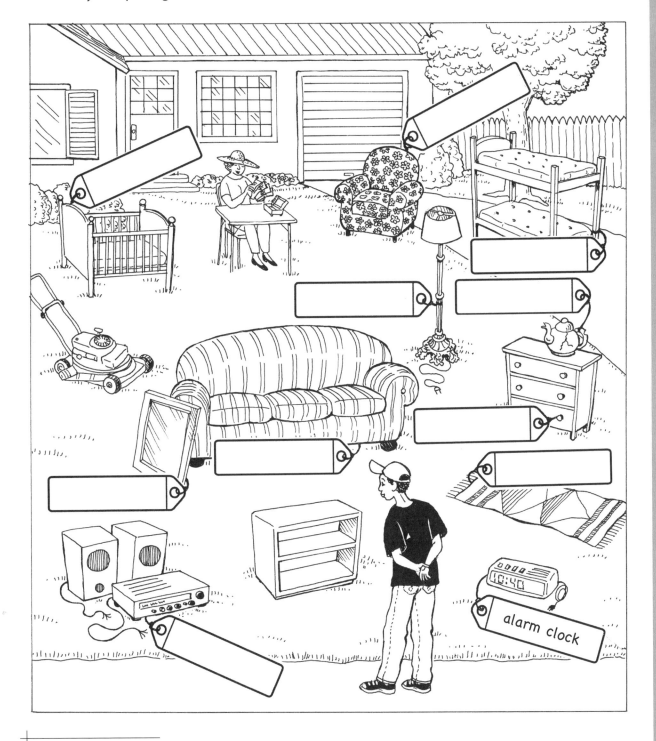

▶ **What's Next?** Work with a partner. Decide on a price for each item in the picture. Then write a conversation between a buyer and a seller. Read your dialogue to the rest of the class.

The Perfect Kitchen A

1. Find a partner with page 49 (B). Don't show your partner this paper.
2. Describe Picture A to your partner. Your partner will draw what you say.
3. Answer your partner's questions.

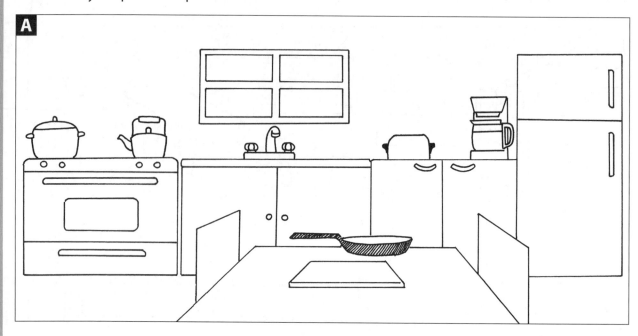

4. Listen to your partner describe Picture B. Draw what you hear. You can ask questions like these: *Is that on the right or on the left? Where is the _____?*
5. When both pictures are complete, compare them.

▶ **What's Next?** Work with a partner. You are cooking dinner for your friends. What do you cook? What items do you need in the kitchen to make the food? Tell your partner about your meal and the kitchen items you use.

Housing

The Perfect Kitchen B

1. Find a partner with page 48 (A). Don't show your partner this paper.
2. Listen to your partner describe Picture A. Draw what you hear. You can ask questions like these: *Is that on the right or on the left? Where is the _____?*

A

B

3. Describe Picture B to your partner. Your partner will draw what you say.
4. Answer your partner's questions.
5. When both pictures are complete, compare them.

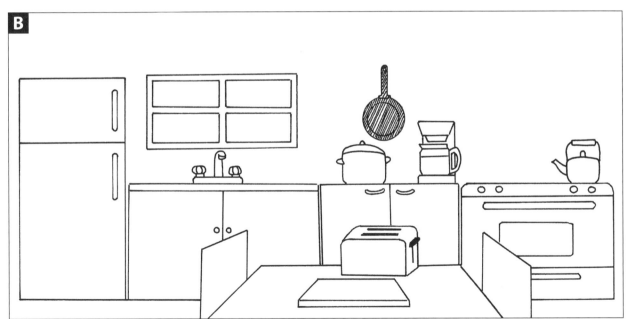

B

▶ **What's Next?** Work with a partner. You are cooking dinner for your friends. What do you cook? What items do you need in the kitchen to make the food? Tell your partner about your meal and the kitchen items you use.

We need that!

1. Work with 3 or 4 classmates. Choose a Recorder.

2. Use the cards to make 10 different sentences or questions. The Recorder writes them down.

HOW	MUCH	MANY	DO
DOES	THE	FAMILY	CHILDREN
NEED	NEEDS	ROOMS	CLOSETS
SOFAS	TOYS	BEDS	SLEEP
SOAP	WATER	.	?

▶ **What's Next?** Share your sentences with the class. Which group made the most sentences? the most questions?

Housing

GRAMMAR ACTIVITY

My Yard A

1. Find a partner with page 52 (B). Look at each other's picture.
2. Find 10 differences with your partner. Write the differences in the chart.

A

	A	B
1.	There's no satellite dish on the roof.	There's a satellite dish on the roof.
2.		
3.		
4.		
5.		
6.		
7.		
8.		
9.		
10.		

▶ **What's Next?** Your teacher will tell you to draw the front of a house or the back yard. When you are finished, find a partner with the opposite side and combine them. Tell your partner about your picture.

My Yard B

1. Find a partner with page 51 (A). Look at each other's picture.
2. Find 10 differences with your partner. Write the differences in the chart.

	A	B
1.	There's no satellite dish on the roof.	There's a satellite dish on the roof.
2.		
3.		
4.		
5.		
6.		
7.		
8.		
9.		
10.		

▶ **What's Next?** Your teacher will tell you to draw the front of a house or the back yard. When you are finished, find a partner with the opposite side and combine them. Tell your partner about your picture.

What's it like at your house?

1. Read the questions. Mark your answers with a ✔.

2. Survey 5 classmates. Write their names, and mark their answer with a ✔.

Do you …	My answers	_____ answers	_____ answers	_____ answers	_____ answers	_____ answers
eat in the kitchen **OR** eat in the dining area?						
study in the living room **OR** study in the bedroom?						
store things in the attic **OR** store things in the basement?						
keep clothes in a dresser **OR** keep clothes in a closet?						
have more paintings **OR** have more photos?						

3. Write sentences about each classmate you surveyed.

> Debbie always eats in the kitchen.

1. _____

2. _____

3. _____

4. _____

5. _____

4. Work with 2 classmates. Read your sentences out loud and compare them.

▶ **What's Next?** Write sentences about your answers.

Housing

Fumi's New Home

1. Work with 2 classmates.
2. Look at the picture. Read the first sentence. Think of more sentences to write about the picture.
3. Take turns writing sentences to continue the story.
4. Check your spelling in the *OPD*.

Fumi shopped for things to put in her living room.

_____

_____

_____

_____

_____

_____

_____

_____

▶ **What's Next?** Work with a partner. You moved to a new home. How would you arrange the furniture and other items in your living room? How would you decorate it? Tell your partner about what you would do.

Finding the Perfect Apartment A

1. Find a partner with page 56 (B). Don't show your partner this paper.

2. Look at A. Ask your partner about the missing information in these classified ads. You can ask questions like these: *What features does the apartment have? How many_____ are there?*

3. Write the missing information.

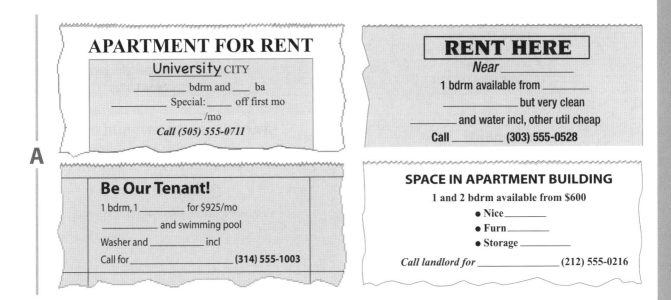

APARTMENT FOR RENT
University CITY
_____ bdrm and ____ ba
_____ Special: ____ off first mo
_____ /mo
Call (505) 555-0711

RENT HERE
Near _____
1 bdrm available from _____
_____ but very clean
_____ and water incl, other util cheap
Call _____ (303) 555-0528

Be Our Tenant!
1 bdrm, 1 _____ for $925/mo
_____ and swimming pool
Washer and _____ incl
Call for _____ **(314) 555-1003**

SPACE IN APARTMENT BUILDING
1 and 2 bdrm available from $600
- Nice _____
- Furn _____
- Storage _____
Call landlord for _____ (212) 555-0216

4. Look at B. Use these classified ads to answer your partner's questions.

5. When you are finished, compare your classified ads with your partner's.

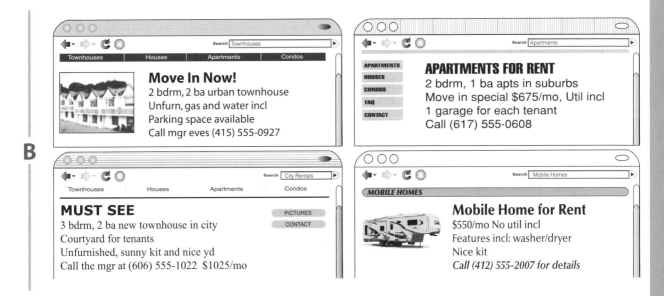

Search | Townhouses
Townhouses | Houses | Apartments | Condos

Move In Now!
2 bdrm, 2 ba urban townhouse
Unfurn, gas and water incl
Parking space available
Call mgr eves (415) 555-0927

Search | Apartments
APARTMENTS | HOUSES | CONDOS | FAQ | CONTACT

APARTMENTS FOR RENT
2 bdrm, 1 ba apts in suburbs
Move in special $675/mo, Util incl
1 garage for each tenant
Call (617) 555-0608

Search | City Rentals
Townhouses | Houses | Apartments | Condos

MUST SEE   PICTURES   CONTACT
3 bdrm, 2 ba new townhouse in city
Courtyard for tenants
Unfurnished, sunny kit and nice yd
Call the mgr at (606) 555-1022 $1025/mo

Search | Mobile Homes
MOBILE HOMES

Mobile Home for Rent
$550/mo No util incl
Features incl: washer/dryer
Nice kit
Call (412) 555-2007 for details

▶ **What's Next?** You are an apartment manager, and you have an apartment to rent. Write a classified ad and post your ad on the board with other students' ads. Which apartment do you want to live in?

Finding the Perfect Apartment B

1. Find a partner with page 55 (A). Don't show your partner this paper.

2. Look at A. Use these classified ads to answer your partner's questions.

A

APARTMENT FOR RENT

UNIVERSITY CITY
Large! 3 bdrm and 1.5 ba
Move in Special: $150 off first mo
$750/mo
Call (505) 555-0711

RENT HERE
Near the city
1 bdrm available from $410
Unfurnished but very clean
Gas and water incl, other util cheap
Call mgr (303) 555-0528

Be Our Tenant!
1 bdrm, 1 ba for $925/mo
Balcony and swimming pool
Washer and dryer incl
Call for rental agreement **(314) 555-1003**

SPACE IN APARTMENT BUILDING
1 and 2 bdrm available from $600
● **Nice lobby**
● **Furn kit**
● **Storage locker**

Call landlord for application **(212) 555-0216**

3. Look at B. Ask your partner about the missing information in these classified ads. You can ask questions like these: *What features does the apartment have? How many_____ are there?*

4. Write the missing information.

5. When you are finished, compare your classified ads with your partner's.

B

Search [Townhouses]
Townhouses | Houses | Apartments | Condos

Move In Now!
2 bdrm, 2 ba urban_____
Unfurn,_____ and _____ incl
_____ available
Call mgr_____(415) 555-0927

Search [Apartments]
APARTMENTS | HOUSES | CONDOS | FAQ | CONTACT

APARTMENTS FOR RENT
2 bdrm, 1 ba apts in _____
Move in special_____,Util_____
1 _____for each tenant
Call (617) 555-0608

Search [City Rentals]
Townhouses | Houses | Apartments | Condos

MUST SEE
3_____ ,_____ ba new townhouse in city
_____ for tenants
Unfurnished, sunny_____and nice _____
Call the mgr at _____ $1025/mo
PICTURES | CONTACT

Search [Mobile Homes]
MOBILE HOMES

Mobile Home for Rent
$550/mo _____util incl
Features incl:_____
Nice_____
Call (412) 555-2007 for details

▶ **What's Next?** You are an apartment manager, and you have an apartment to rent. Write a classified ad and post your ad on the board with other students' ads. Which apartment do you want to live in?

Spring Cleaning!

1. Work with 3 classmates.

2. Write the character next to each line.

3. Choose your character. Write other lines you could say.

4. Practice saying the lines. Act out the role play.

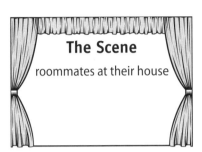

The Scene

roommates at their house

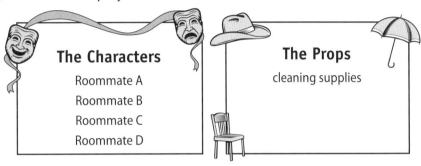

The Characters

Roommate A
Roommate B
Roommate C
Roommate D

The Props

cleaning supplies

The Script

<u>Roommate A:</u>	The house is so dirty. Let's do some housework!
_____	You're right. The house *is* dirty! I can wash <u>the dishes</u>.*
_____	Oh, you should use <u>rubber gloves</u>.
_____	I'll <u>mop</u> the floor. I like doing that.
_____	<u>The bucket</u> is in <u>the kitchen closet</u>.
_____	We need to <u>fix</u> things, too.
_____	Yeah, the <u>lock</u> is broken.
_____	I'll call <u>a locksmith</u>.
_____	And the <u>faucet</u> is <u>leaking</u>!
_____	Let's call <u>a plumber</u> for that.
_____	Do we need to do anything else?

*You can use other vocabulary for the underlined words.

▶ **What's Next?** Write a list of housework you need to do at your home. For each job, write the cleaning supplies you need or the repair people you need to call.

An Apartment or a House?

1. Think about reasons to live in an apartment or live in a house.
2. Read the statements in the chart.
3. Write 2 more statements in the chart.
4. If the statement shows that living in an apartment is a good idea, ✔ that column. If the statement shows that living in a house is a good idea, ✔ that column.

Statements	living in an apartment	living in a house
Apartments are usually cheaper than houses.		
A landlord can fix broken things for you.		
Neighbors can't hear you very well.		
You can have your own yard and garden.		
An apartment usually comes with a stove.		
Some utilities are often included.		
It's easier to have a pet.		
You can have a private front door.		
There is more space to put your things.		
You can meet other tenants and become friends.		

5. Work with a partner. Compare your ideas.
6. Write your and your partner's ideas.

I think that living in a/an _____ is a good idea because _____

_____

My partner thinks that living in a/an _____ is a good idea because _____

_____

▶ **What's Next?** Take a stand. Your teacher will tell you where to stand if you support living in an apartment and where to stand if you support living in a house.

Food

Fruit and Vegetables

1. Work with a partner. Cut apart the cards.

2. Write the Word List words on the back of the cards.

3. Student A: Show the picture to your partner.
Student B: Say the word or phrase.

4. Take turns.

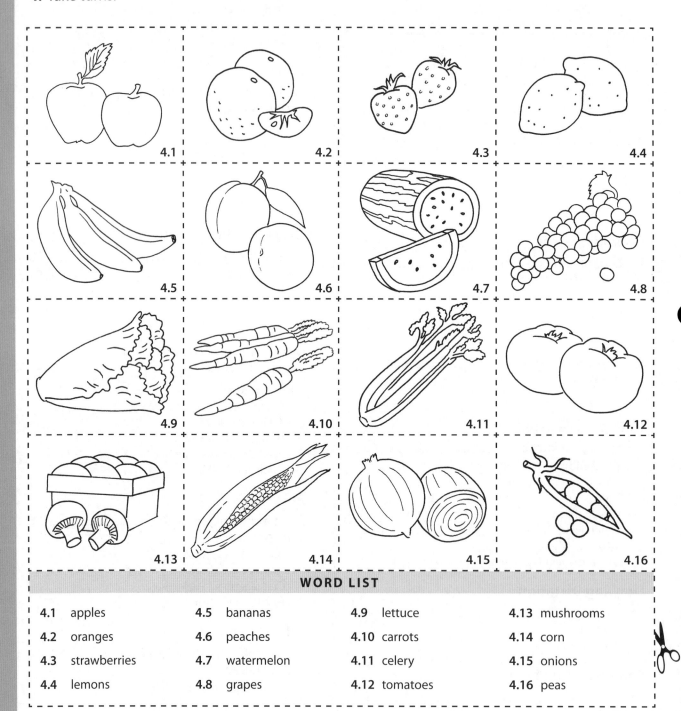

WORD LIST			
4.1 apples	**4.5** bananas	**4.9** lettuce	**4.13** mushrooms
4.2 oranges	**4.6** peaches	**4.10** carrots	**4.14** corn
4.3 strawberries	**4.7** watermelon	**4.11** celery	**4.15** onions
4.4 lemons	**4.8** grapes	**4.12** tomatoes	**4.16** peas

Foods

1. Work with a partner. Cut apart the cards.
2. Write the Word List words on the back of the cards.
3. Student A: Show the picture to your partner.
   Student B: Say the word or phrase.
4. Take turns.

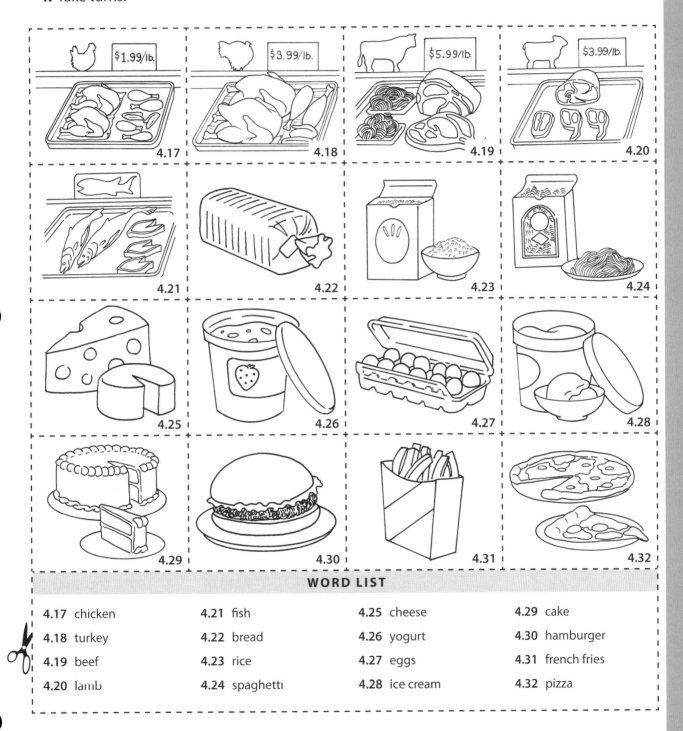

WORD LIST

4.17 chicken	4.21 fish	4.25 cheese	4.29 cake
4.18 turkey	4.22 bread	4.26 yogurt	4.30 hamburger
4.19 beef	4.23 rice	4.27 eggs	4.31 french fries
4.20 lamb	4.24 spaghetti	4.28 ice cream	4.32 pizza

Food

Food

In the Kitchen

1. Work with 3 classmates. Cut apart the cards. Put them face down in a pile.
2. Student A: Pick a card. Describe the word or phrase on the card.
   Students B, C, and D: Guess the word or phrase.
3. The first student to guess correctly keeps the card.
4. Take turns.

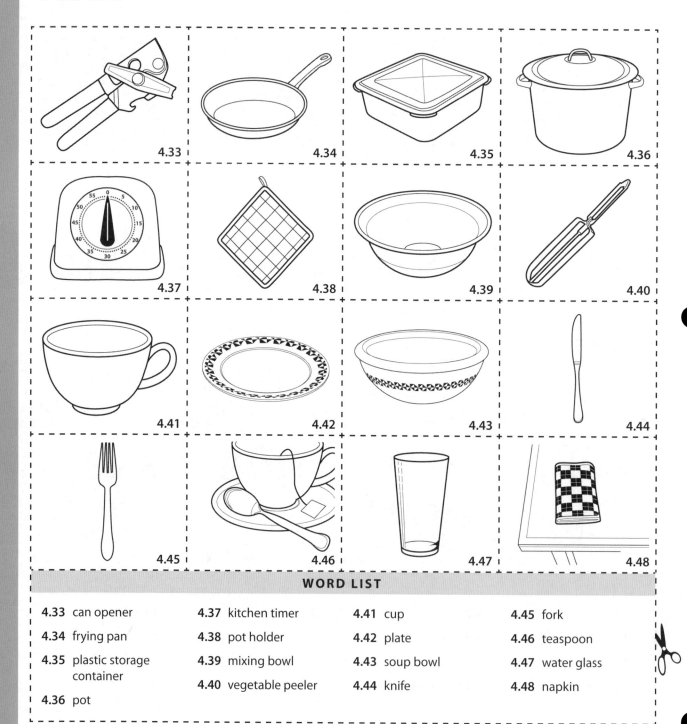

4.33	4.34	4.35	4.36
4.37	4.38	4.39	4.40
4.41	4.42	4.43	4.44
4.45	4.46	4.47	4.48

WORD LIST

4.33 can opener	**4.37** kitchen timer	**4.41** cup	**4.45** fork
4.34 frying pan	**4.38** pot holder	**4.42** plate	**4.46** teaspoon
4.35 plastic storage container	**4.39** mixing bowl	**4.43** soup bowl	**4.47** water glass
4.36 pot	**4.40** vegetable peeler	**4.44** knife	**4.48** napkin

Restaurant and Cooking Verbs

1. Work with 3 classmates. Cut apart the cards. Put the cards face down in a pile.
2. Student A: Pick a card. Silently act out the action.
   Student B: Ask *What is he / she doing?*
   Students C and D: Answer the question using the present continuous. (*She is seating a customer.*)
   Student B: Write what your classmates say.
3. Take turns.

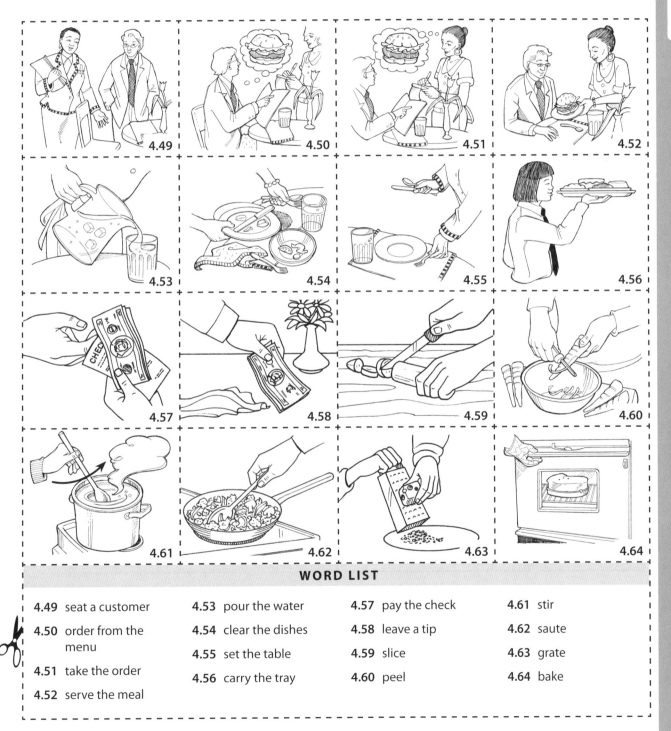

WORD LIST			
4.49 seat a customer	**4.53** pour the water	**4.57** pay the check	**4.61** stir
4.50 order from the menu	**4.54** clear the dishes	**4.58** leave a tip	**4.62** saute
	4.55 set the table	**4.59** slice	**4.63** grate
4.51 take the order	**4.56** carry the tray	**4.60** peel	**4.64** bake
4.52 serve the meal			

Grocery Shopping Grid

1. Use this grid with the picture cards on page 65.
2. Student A: Put one picture on each square on the grid. Don't show your partner your grid.
    Use the picture and the square to tell your partner a sentence.
    (*The jam is in aisle 1A.*)

    Student B: Listen to your partner. Check what you heard.
    (*Did you say the jam is in aisle 1A?*)
    Put the picture on the correct square on the grid.

3. When the grids are full, compare them. If they are the same, change roles. If not, try again.

aisle 1A	aisle 1B	aisle 2A	aisle 2B
aisle 3A	aisle 3B	aisle 4A	aisle 4B
aisle 5A	aisle 5B	aisle 6A	aisle 6B
aisle 7A	aisle 7B	aisle 8A	aisle 8B

Grocery Shopping Cards

1. Use these picture cards with the grid on page 64.

2. Work with a partner. Cut apart the cards.

WORD LIST			
4.65 jam	**4.69** flour	**4.73** margarine	**4.77** candy bars
4.66 cereal	**4.70** soup	**4.74** potato chips	**4.78** oil
4.67 milk	**4.71** soda	**4.75** tuna	**4.79** plastic wrap
4.68 cookies	**4.72** sour cream	**4.76** apple juice	**4.80** sugar

Food

GRAMMAR ACTIVITY

Food

What's in your kitchen?

1. Work with 2 classmates.
2. Label what you see in the picture. Take turns.
3. Check your spelling in the *OPD*.

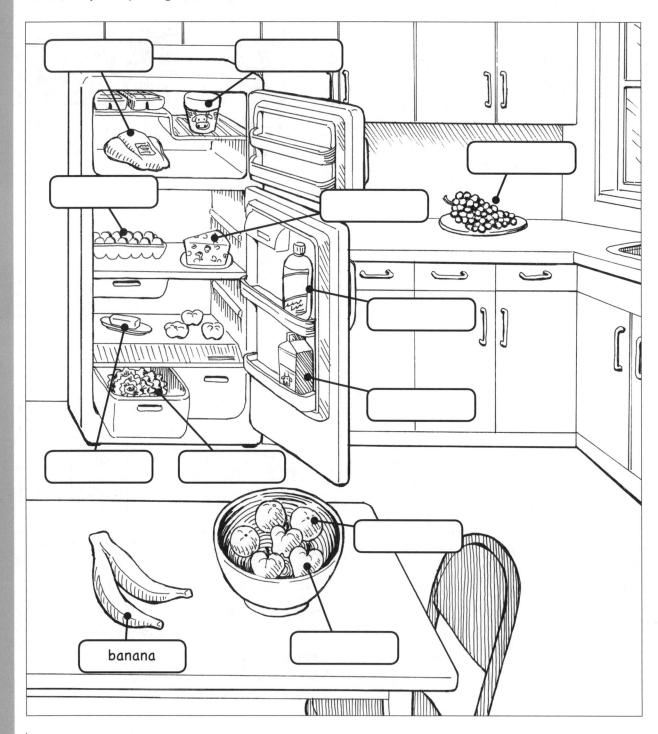

banana

▶ **What's Next?** Your teacher will draw an open refrigerator on the board. Take turns telling classmate volunteers what to draw on the shelves or in the door.

Let's set the table A

1. Find a partner with page 68 (B). Don't show your partner this paper.

2. Describe Picture A to your partner. Your partner will draw what you say.

3. Answer your partner's questions.

4. Listen to your partner describe Picture B. Draw what you hear. You can ask questions like these: *Where is the _____? Does it go on the left or the right?*

5. When both pictures are complete, compare them.

▶ **What's Next?** How are the place settings and dishes for a meal arranged on a table in your country or culture? Share your information with the class.

Let's set the table B

1. Find a partner with page 67 (A). Don't show your partner this paper.
2. Listen to your partner describe Picture A. Draw what you hear. You can ask questions like these: *Where is the _____? Does it go on the left or the right?*

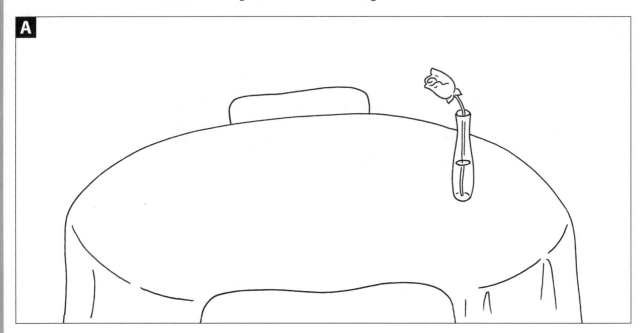

3. Describe Picture B to your partner. Your partner will draw what you say.
4. Answer your partner's questions.
5. When both pictures are complete, compare them.

▶ **What's Next?** How are the place settings and dishes for a meal arranged on a table in your country or culture? Share your information with the class.

I'm hungry!

1. Work with 3 or 4 classmates. Choose a Recorder.

2. Use the cards to make 10 different sentences or questions. The Recorder writes them down.

I	I'D	YOU	CAN
HAVE	LIKE	DO	WANT
A	SOME	FRENCH FRIES	RICE
PIZZA	ROAST CHICKEN	CHEESEBURGER	SALAD
SOUP	STEAMED VEGETABLES	.	?

▶ **What's Next?** Share your sentences with the class. Which group made the most sentences? the most questions?

What did you buy? A

1. Find a partner with page 71 (B). Look at each other's picture.

2. Find 10 differences with your partner. Write the differences in the chart.

A	**B**
1. There are three cans of pinto beans.	There are two cans of pinto beans.
2.	
3.	
4.	
5.	
6.	
7.	
8.	
9.	
10.	

▶ **What's Next?** Work with a partner. What are your favorite foods? Write a shopping list, and share it with your partner. What foods are the same? What foods are different?

What did you buy? B

1. Find a partner with page 70 (A). Look at each other's picture.

2. Find 10 differences with your partner. Write the differences in the chart.

B

A	B
1. There are three cans of pinto beans.	There are two cans of pinto beans.
2.	
3.	
4.	
5.	
6.	
7.	
8.	
9.	
10.	

▶ **What's Next?** Work with a partner. What are your favorite foods? Write a shopping list, and share it with your partner. What foods are the same? What foods are different?

What do you want for dinner?

1. Read the questions. Mark your answers with a ✔.

2. Survey 5 classmates. Write their names, and mark their answers with a ✔.

Do you prefer …	My answers	_____ answers	_____ answers	_____ answers	_____ answers	_____ answers
roasted chicken OR fried chicken?						
scrambled eggs OR hardboiled eggs?						
cooked carrots OR raw carrots?						
mashed potatoes OR baked potatoes?						
wheat bread OR white bread?						
fresh fruit OR canned fruit?						
coffee OR tea?						

3. Write sentences about each classmate you surveyed.

Mohamed prefers roasted chicken to fried chicken.

1. _____

2. _____

3. _____

4. _____

5. _____

4. Work with 2 classmates. Read your sentences out loud and compare them.

▶ **What's Next?** Write sentences about your answers.

What a great meal!

1. Work with 2 classmates.
2. Look at the picture. Read the first sentence. Think of more sentences to write about the picture.
3. Take turns writing sentences to continue the story.
4. Check your spelling in the *OPD*.

The Lopez family had a delicious meal last night.

_____

_____

_____

_____

_____

_____

_____

_____

_____

▶ **What's Next?** Continue working with your group. Write a shopping list for the meal in the picture. Share your list with the class.

Food

How much do I need? A

1. Find a partner with page 75 (B). Don't show your partner this paper.

2. Look at A. Ask your partner about the missing information in this recipe. You can ask questions like these: *How much _____ do I need? How many _____ do I need?*

3. Write the missing information.

A

COCOA-COCONUT-BERRY BALLS (makes 50 cookies)

__2c__ vanilla wafers　　　____ jam

____ powdered sugar　　____ chopped nuts

____ cocoa　　　　　　　____ shredded coconut

1. Crush the vanilla wafers and put them in a large bowl.
2. _____ the cocoa to the wafers.
3. _____ the coconut, jam and chopped nuts.
4. Make small balls of the mixture and put them on a plate.
5. Cocoa-Coconut-Berry Balls can stay in the refrigerator for a _____.

A

4. Look at B. Use this recipe to answer your partner's questions.

5. When you are finished, compare your recipes with your partner's.

B

FRUIT SALAD (serves 6)

1/2 lb. grapes　　　　3 peaches or pears

3 apples　　　　　　1 15-oz. can sliced pineapple

1/2 c. yogurt　　　　1/4 c. raisins

1. Wash all the fruit.
2. Chop the apples.
3. Slice the peaches or pears.
4. Cut up the pineapple into bite-size pieces.
5. Put all the fruit into a large bowl.
6. Mix in the yogurt and add the raisins.
7. Refrigerate for 1/2 hour. Serves 6.

▶ **What's Next?** Which kitchen utensils will you need to make these recipes? Make a list and tell a classmate.

How much do I need? B

1. Find a partner with page 74 (A). Don't show your partner this paper.
2. Look at A. Use this recipe to answer your partner's questions.

A

> ## COCOA-COCONUT-BERRY BALLS (makes 50 cookies)
>
> | | |
> |---|---|
> | 2 c. vanilla wafers | 3 Tbs. jam |
> | 1/2 c. powdered sugar | 1/4 c. chopped nuts |
> | 3 Tbs. cocoa | 1/2 c shredded coconut |
>
> 1. Crush the vanilla wafers and put them in a large bowl.
> 2. Add the cocoa to the wafers.
> 3. Mix in the coconut, jam and chopped nuts.
> 4. Make small balls of the mixture and put them on a plate.
> 5. Cocoa-Coconut-Berry Balls can stay in the refrigerator for a week.

3. Look at B. Ask your partner about the missing information in this recipe. You can ask questions like these: *How much _____ do I need? How many _____ do I need?*
4. Write the missing information.
5. When you are finished, compare your recipes with your partner's.

B

> ## FRUIT SALAD (serves 6)
>
> | | |
> |---|---|
> | <u>1/2 lb</u> grapes | _____ peaches or pears |
> | _____ apples | _____ sliced pineapple |
> | _____ yogurt | _____ raisins |
>
> 1. Wash all the fruit.
> 2. _____ apples.
> 3. _____ the peaches or pears.
> 4. _____ pineapple into bite-size pieces.
> 5. Put all the fruit into a large bowl.
> 6. _____ in the yogurt and add the raisins.
> 7. Refrigerate for 1/2 hour. Serves 6.

▶ **What's Next?** Which kitchen utensils will you need to make these recipes? Make a list and tell a classmate.

Don't forget to get carrots!

1. Work with 3 classmates.

2. Write the character next to each line.

3. Choose your character. Write other lines you could say.

4. Practice saying the lines. Act out the role play.

The Scene
family sitting in their
kitchen making a
grocery list

The Characters
Mom
Dad
Teenager
Child

The Props
empty food packages
paper
a pencil or a pen

The Script

Mom: We need some food! Let's see… We need to get <u>a loaf of bread</u>.*

_____   We also need to buy some <u>pasta</u>.

_____   Good idea. Let's get some <u>chicken</u>, too.

_____   Can we get some <u>ice cream</u>?

_____   You don't need any <u>ice cream</u>.

_____   Oh, don't forget to get <u>carrots</u>. Mm, I love <u>carrots</u>.

_____   But I hate <u>carrots</u>! Can we get <u>potato chips</u> instead?

_____   No, we're not buying any more <u>snack food</u>!

_____   How about some <u>pizza</u>? Let's put it on the list.

_____   OK. Let's get <u>a cheese and mushroom pizza</u>.

_____   What else do we need to buy?

*You can use other vocabulary for the underlined words.

▶ **What's Next?** Continue working with your group. Plan a meal that all four of the family members will like. Include a dessert and beverages.

Homecooked Meals or Fast Food?

1. Think about reasons to eat homecooked meals or fast food.
2. Read the statements in the chart.
3. Write 2 more statements in the chart.
4. If the statement shows that eating homecooked meals is a good idea, ✔ that column.
   If the statement shows that eating fast food is a good idea, ✔ that column.

Statements	eating homecooked meals	eating fast food
Fast food can be very cheap.		
You can order and eat while you are traveling in a car.		
Fast food can have a lot of salt and fat.		
Everyone can order their favorite food.		
You don't have to cook or clean up.		
You can make special foods from your country.		
You can cook and eat any time you want.		
You and your family can enjoy cooking together.		
You can make sure all the ingredients are fresh.		
You can make sure food is prepared safely.		

5. Work with a partner. Compare your ideas.
6. Write your and your partner's ideas.

   I think that eating _____ is a good idea because _____

   _____

   My partner thinks that eating _____ is a good idea because _____

   _____

▶ **What's Next?** Work as a class. How many students prefer eating homemade food? fast food? Draw a bar graph on the board. Then discuss the results.

The Good, the Bad, the Ugly!

1. Work with a partner. Cut apart the cards.
2. Write the Word List words on the back of the cards.
3. Student A: Show the picture to your partner.
   Student B: Say the word or phrase.
4. Take turns.

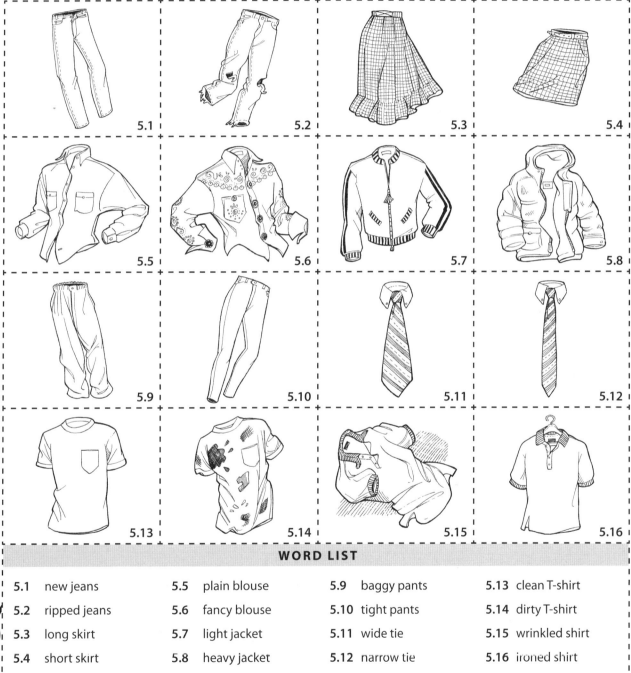

WORD LIST			
5.1 new jeans	5.5 plain blouse	5.9 baggy pants	5.13 clean T-shirt
5.2 ripped jeans	5.6 fancy blouse	5.10 tight pants	5.14 dirty T-shirt
5.3 long skirt	5.7 light jacket	5.11 wide tie	5.15 wrinkled shirt
5.4 short skirt	5.8 heavy jacket	5.12 narrow tie	5.16 ironed shirt

Make yourself look better!

1. Work with a partner. Cut apart the cards.
2. Write the Word List words on the back of the cards.
3. Student A: Show the picture to your partner.
   Student B: Say the word or phrase.
4. Take turns.

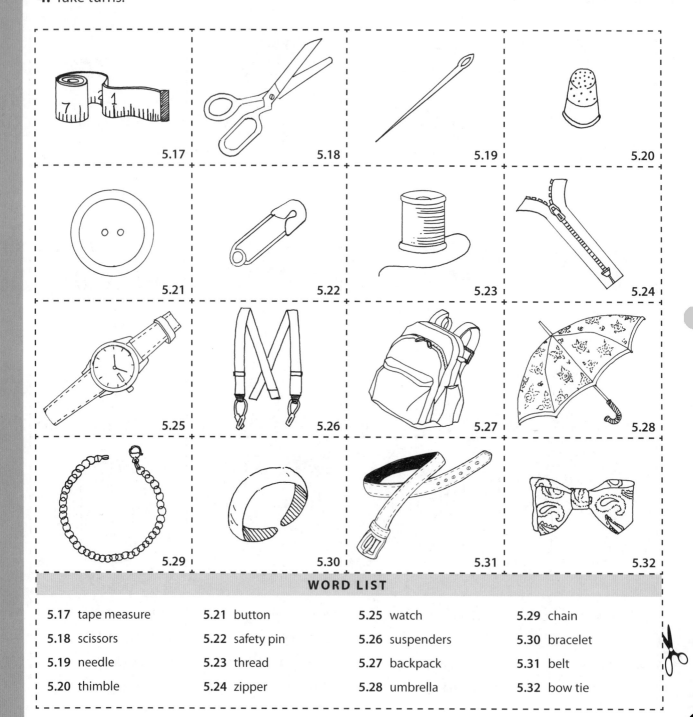

5.17	5.18	5.19	5.20
5.21	5.22	5.23	5.24
5.25	5.26	5.27	5.28
5.29	5.30	5.31	5.32

WORD LIST

5.17 tape measure	5.21 button	5.25 watch	5.29 chain
5.18 scissors	5.22 safety pin	5.26 suspenders	5.30 bracelet
5.19 needle	5.23 thread	5.27 backpack	5.31 belt
5.20 thimble	5.24 zipper	5.28 umbrella	5.32 bow tie

What should I wear to work?

1. Work with 3 classmates. Cut apart the cards. Put them face down in a pile.
2. Student A: Pick a card. Describe the word or phrase on the card.
   Students B, C, and D: Guess the word or phrase.
3. The first student to guess correctly keeps the card.
4. Take turns.

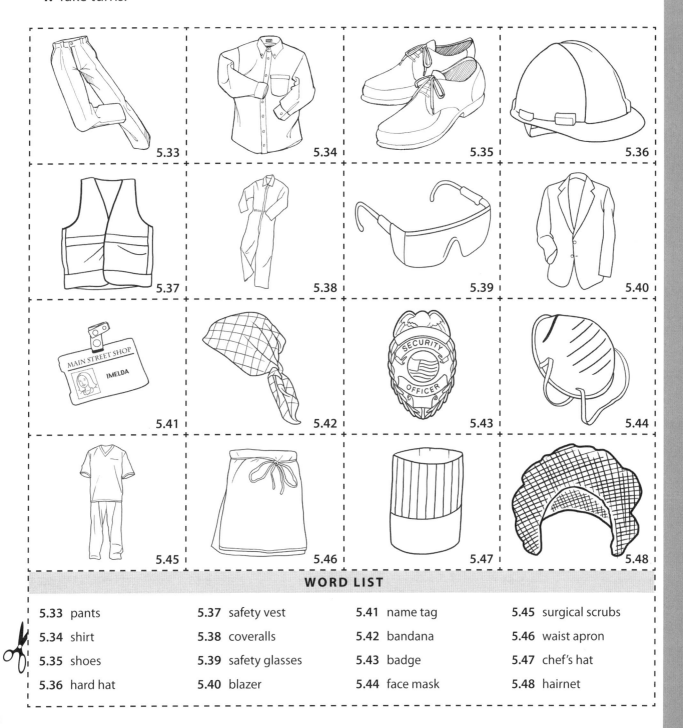

5.33	5.34	5.35	5.36
5.37	5.38	5.39	5.40
5.41	5.42	5.43	5.44
5.45	5.46	5.47	5.48

WORD LIST

5.33 pants	5.37 safety vest	5.41 name tag	5.45 surgical scrubs
5.34 shirt	5.38 coveralls	5.42 bandana	5.46 waist apron
5.35 shoes	5.39 safety glasses	5.43 badge	5.47 chef's hat
5.36 hard hat	5.40 blazer	5.44 face mask	5.48 hairnet

Clothing

What are you doing?

1. Work with 3 classmates. Cut apart the cards. Put the cards face down in a pile.

2. Student A: Pick a card. Silently act out the action.

     Student B: Ask *What is he / she doing?*

     Students C and D: Answer the question using the present continuous. (*He is tying shoelaces.*)

     Student B: Write what your classmates say.

3. Take turns.

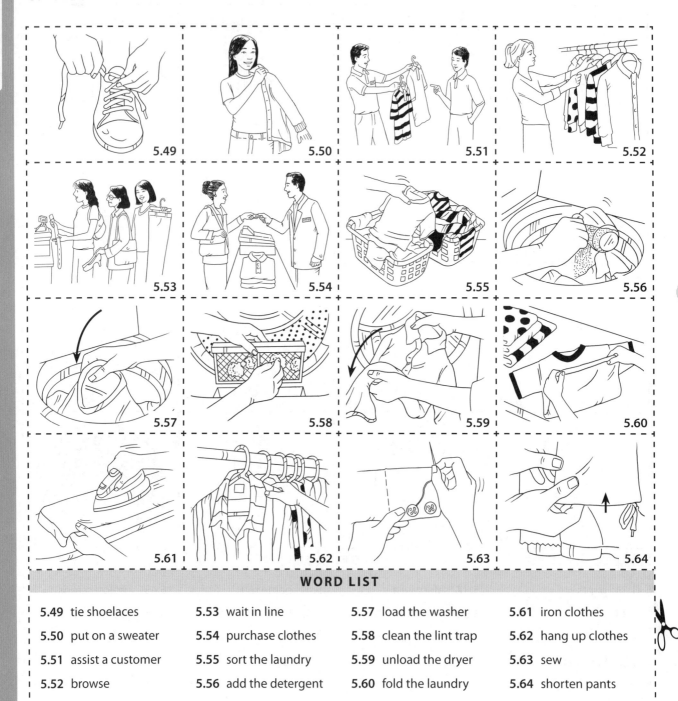

5.49	5.50	5.51	5.52
5.53	5.54	5.55	5.56
5.57	5.58	5.59	5.60
5.61	5.62	5.63	5.64

WORD LIST

5.49 tie shoelaces	**5.53** wait in line	**5.57** load the washer	**5.61** iron clothes
5.50 put on a sweater	**5.54** purchase clothes	**5.58** clean the lint trap	**5.62** hang up clothes
5.51 assist a customer	**5.55** sort the laundry	**5.59** unload the dryer	**5.63** sew
5.52 browse	**5.56** add the detergent	**5.60** fold the laundry	**5.64** shorten pants

How much does it cost? Grid

1. Use this grid with the picture cards on page 84.

2. Student A: Put one picture on each square on the grid. Don't show your partner your grid.
   Use the picture and the square to tell your partner a sentence.
   (*The parka costs $75.50.*)

   Student B: Listen to your partner. Check what you heard.
   (*Did you say the parka costs $75.50?*)
   Put the picture on the correct square on the grid.

3. When the grids are full, compare them. If they are the same, change roles. If not, try again.

$14.99	$19.99	$29.99	$34.99
$20.00	$30.00	$40.00	$100.00
$27.50	$38.50	$42.50	$75.50
$13.99	$16.99	$66.99	$150.99

Clothing

GRAMMAR ACTIVITY

Clothing

GRAMMAR ACTIVITY

How much does it cost? Cards

1. Use these picture cards with the grid on page 83.

2. Work with a partner. Cut apart the cards.

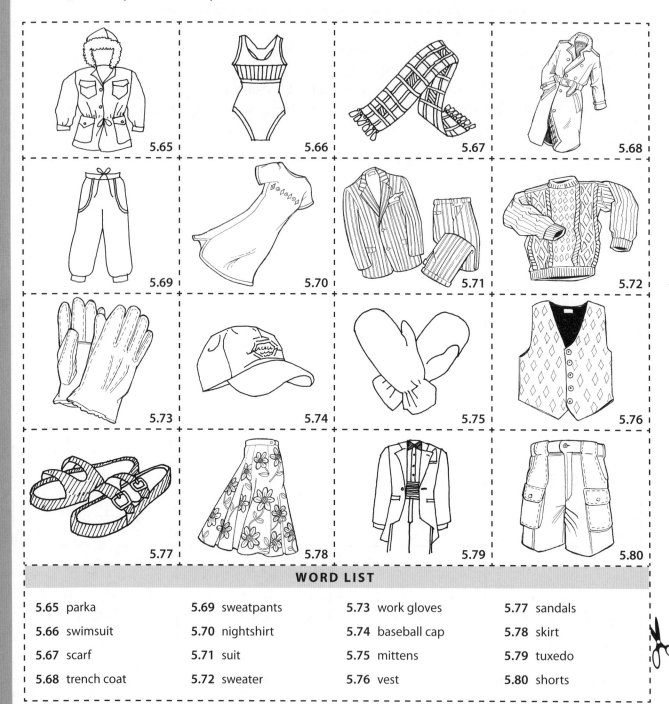

5.65	5.66	5.67	5.68
5.69	5.70	5.71	5.72
5.73	5.74	5.75	5.76
5.77	5.78	5.79	5.80

WORD LIST

5.65 parka	**5.69** sweatpants	**5.73** work gloves	**5.77** sandals
5.66 swimsuit	**5.70** nightshirt	**5.74** baseball cap	**5.78** skirt
5.67 scarf	**5.71** suit	**5.75** mittens	**5.79** tuxedo
5.68 trench coat	**5.72** sweater	**5.76** vest	**5.80** shorts

Looking Good at the Park

1. Work with 2 classmates.
2. Label what you see in the picture. Take turns.
3. Check your spelling in the *OPD*.

polo shirt

▶ **What's Next?** Work with a partner. Draw figures of people on a piece of paper. Take turns telling each other clothing items and accessories to draw on them.

What's on your clothesline? A

1. Find a partner with page 87 (B). Don't show your partner this paper.
2. Describe Picture A to your partner. Your partner will draw what you say.
3. Answer your partner's questions.

4. Listen to your partner describe Picture B. Draw what you hear. You can ask questions like these: *What size is the _____? What kind of _____ is it?*
5. When both pictures are complete, compare them.

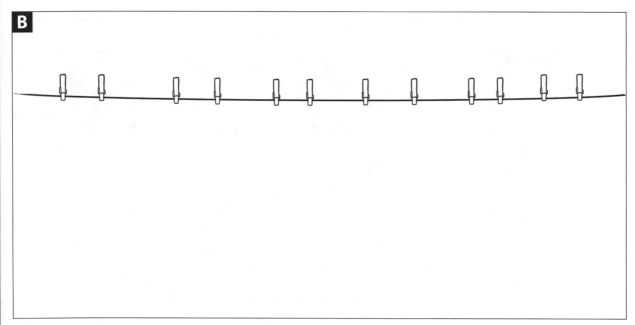

▶ **What's Next?** Describe items on a clothesline to your teacher. Your teacher will draw what you say. Correct your teacher's mistakes.

What's on your clothesline? B

1. Find a partner with page 86 (A). Don't show your partner this paper.
2. Listen to your partner describe Picture A. Draw what you hear. You can ask questions like these: *What size is the _____? What kind of _____ is it?*

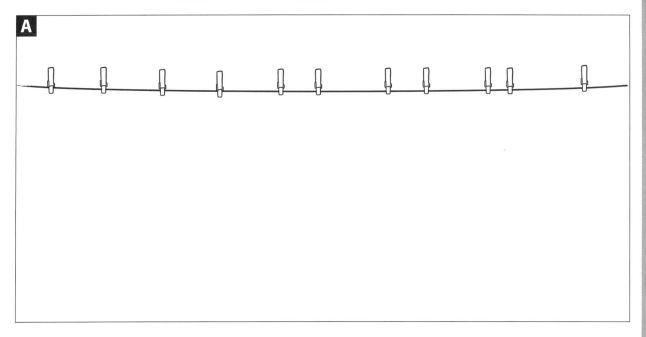

3. Describe Picture B to your partner. Your partner will draw what you say.
4. Answer your partner's questions.
5. When both pictures are complete, compare them.

B

▶ **What's Next?** Describe items on a clothesline to your teacher. Your teacher will draw what you say. Correct your teacher's mistakes.

What are you wearing?

1. Work with 3 or 4 classmates. Choose a Recorder.

2. Use the cards to make 10 different sentences or questions. The Recorder writes them down.

HE	SHE	WHO	YOU
IS	ARE	WEARING	WHAT
A	LONG	LARGE	V-NECK
CREWNECK	SLEEVELESS	JACKET	PANTS
SHIRT	SWEATER	.	?

▶ **What's Next?** Share your sentences with the class. Which group made the most sentences? the most questions?

A Busy Night of Laundry A

1. Find a partner with page 90 (B). Look at each other's picture.

2. Find 10 differences with your partner. Write the differences in the chart.

A

A		B	
1.	The laundry basket is on the floor.	The laundry basket is on the dryer.	
2.			
3.			
4.			
5.			
6.			
7.			
8.			
9.			
10.			

▶ **What's Next?** You are starting your own laundry business. How much will your cleaning services (like sorting, folding, ironing, and hanging) cost? Talk about your business with your classmates.

A Busy Night of Laundry B

1. Find a partner with page 89 (A). Look at each other's picture.
2. Find 10 differences with your partner. Write the differences in the chart.

	A		B
1.	The laundry basket is on the floor.		The laundry basket is on the dryer.
2.			
3.			
4.			
5.			
6.			
7.			
8.			
9.			
10.			

▶ **What's Next?** You are starting your own laundry business. How much will your cleaning services (like sorting, folding, ironing, and hanging) cost? Talk about your business with your classmates.

What's your style?

1. Read the questions. Mark your answers with a ✔.

2. Survey 5 classmates. Write their names, and mark their answers with a ✔.

Do you prefer …	My answers	_____ answers	_____ answers	_____ answers	_____ answers	_____ answers
long-sleeved shirts **OR** short-sleeved shirts?						
pullover sweaters **OR** cardigan sweaters?						
solid t-shirts **OR** print t-shirts?						
jeans **OR** slacks?						
turtlenecks **OR** V-necks?						
mittens **OR** gloves?						
tight clothes **OR** loose clothes?						

3. Write sentences about each classmate you surveyed.

> Juan prefers short-sleeved shirts to long-sleeved shirts.

1. _____

2. _____

3. _____

4. _____

5. _____

4. Work with 2 classmates. Read your sentences out loud and compare them.

▶ **What's Next?** Write sentences about your answers.

Clothing

GRAMMAR ACTIVITY

Clothing

I need to go shopping

1. Work with 2 classmates.

2. Look at the picture. Read the first sentence. Think of more sentences to write about the picture.

3. Take turns writing sentences to continue the story.

4. Check your spelling in the *OPD*.

Pilar   Rita   Victor   Michael   Aiko   Richard

Pilar needs an evening gown because she is going to a dance.

_____

_____

_____

_____

_____

_____

_____

_____

_____

▶ **What's Next?** Continue working with your group. What are your plans for this weekend? What will you wear? Why?

▶ **Information Exchange A** (See page xxiii for Teacher's Notes.)

OPD pages 98–99, 101

Clothing

Read Before Washing A

1. Find a partner with page 94 (B). Don't show your partner this paper.

2. Look at A. Ask your partner about the missing information in these clothing labels. You can ask questions like these: *What size is the _____? What material is the _____ made from?*

3. Write the missing information.

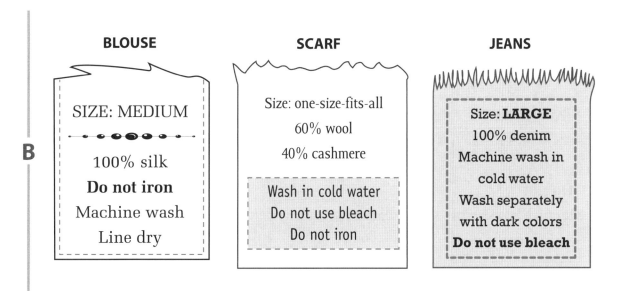

A

SWEATER

SIZE: <u>EXTRA SMALL</u>

55% _____

45% wool

DO NOT _____

_____ **ONLY**

SHIRT

Size: Medium

100% _____

Wash in hot water

_____ and _____

with whites only

_____ up to dry

PANTS

SIZE: _____

50% LINEN

50% _____

Wash in _____ water

No _____

Line dry

4. Look at B. Use these clothing labels to answer your partner's questions.

5. When you are finished, compare your clothing labels with your partner's.

B

BLOUSE

SIZE: MEDIUM

100% silk

Do not iron

Machine wash

Line dry

SCARF

Size: one-size-fits-all

60% wool

40% cashmere

Wash in cold water
Do not use bleach
Do not iron

JEANS

Size: **LARGE**
100% denim
Machine wash in
cold water
Wash separately
with dark colors
Do not use bleach

▶ **What's Next?** Work with a partner. Ask questions about where they do laundry, how often they do it, what kinds of clothes they wash, and what kinds of clothes they dry clean.

A

Clothing

Read Before Washing B

1. Find a partner with page 93 (A). Don't show your partner this paper.
2. Look at A. Use these clothing labels to answer your partner's questions.

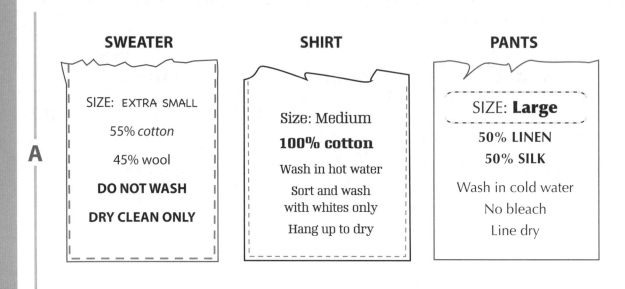

A

SWEATER

SIZE: EXTRA SMALL

55% *cotton*

45% wool

DO NOT WASH

DRY CLEAN ONLY

SHIRT

Size: Medium

100% cotton

Wash in hot water

Sort and wash with whites only

Hang up to dry

PANTS

SIZE: **Large**

50% LINEN

50% SILK

Wash in cold water

No bleach

Line dry

3. Look at B. Ask your partner about the missing information in these clothing labels. You can ask questions like these: *What size is the ____? What material is the ____ made from?*
4. Write the missing information.
5. When you are finished, compare your clothing labels with your partner's.

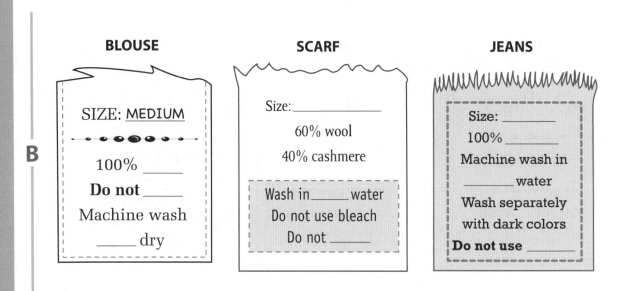

B

BLOUSE

SIZE: MEDIUM

100% _____

Do not _____

Machine wash

_____ dry

SCARF

Size: _____

60% wool

40% cashmere

Wash in _____ water

Do not use bleach

Do not _____

JEANS

Size: _____

100% _____

Machine wash in _____ water

Wash separately with dark colors

Do not use _____

▶ **What's Next?** Work with a partner. Ask questions about where they do laundry, how often they do it, what kinds of clothes they wash, and what kinds of clothes they dry clean.

Lacy's Alterations Shop

1. Work with 2 classmates.

2. Write the character next to each line.

3. Choose your character. Write other lines you could say.

4. Practice saying the lines. Act out the role play.

The Scene

an alterations store

The Characters

Customer A

Customer B

Tailor or dressmaker

The Props

clothing items
a few sewing items

The Script

Customer A: Can you help me? I bought a jacket, but it's too tight.*

_____   Let me see. Yes, I can let it out for you.

_____   That's great.

_____   And there's a button missing, too.

_____   Really? You're right.

_____   I can sew it on for you.

_____   Thanks!

_____   Excuse me, I'd like to shorten these pants.

_____   Sure, could you put them on, please?

_____   OK. The zipper is broken, too.

_____   I can fix that. Let me get my tape measure.

_____   _____

_____   _____

_____   _____

*You can use other vocabulary for the underlined words.

▶ **What's Next?** You are going on vacation. Decide where you will go and what clothes you need. Make a list of 20 clothing or accessory items. After you finish, tell the class where you are going and what items you are taking.

School Uniforms—Yes or No?

1. Think about reasons to wear school uniforms or not to wear school uniforms.
2. Read the statements in the chart.
3. Write 2 more statements in the chart.
4. If the statement shows that wearing school uniforms is a good idea, ✔ that column. If the statement shows that wearing school uniforms is a bad idea, ✔ that column.

Statements	good idea	bad idea
Young people like to wear the latest fashion styles.		
Some parents cannot afford to buy many clothes for their children.		
Some students enjoy wearing special school colors.		
Some students don't want to decide what to wear each day.		
Gangs identify their members by special clothes or colors.		
Some teachers say their students study better in uniforms.		
Wearing different clothes allows students to be individuals.		
Many students don't like to wear the same style and color every day.		
Some students feel bad if they don't have nice clothes like their friends.		
Uniforms can be uncomfortable.		

5. Work with a partner. Compare your ideas.
6. Write your and your partner's ideas.

I think that wearing school uniforms is a _____ idea because _____

_____

My partner thinks that wearing school uniforms is a _____ idea because

_____

▶ **What's Next?** Take a stand. Your teacher will tell you where to stand if you support wearing school uniforms and where to stand if you don't support wearing school uniforms.

Health

Parts of the Body

1. Work with a partner. Cut apart the cards.
2. Write the Word List words on the back of the cards.
3. Student A: Show the picture to your partner.
   Student B: Say the word or phrase.
4. Take turns.

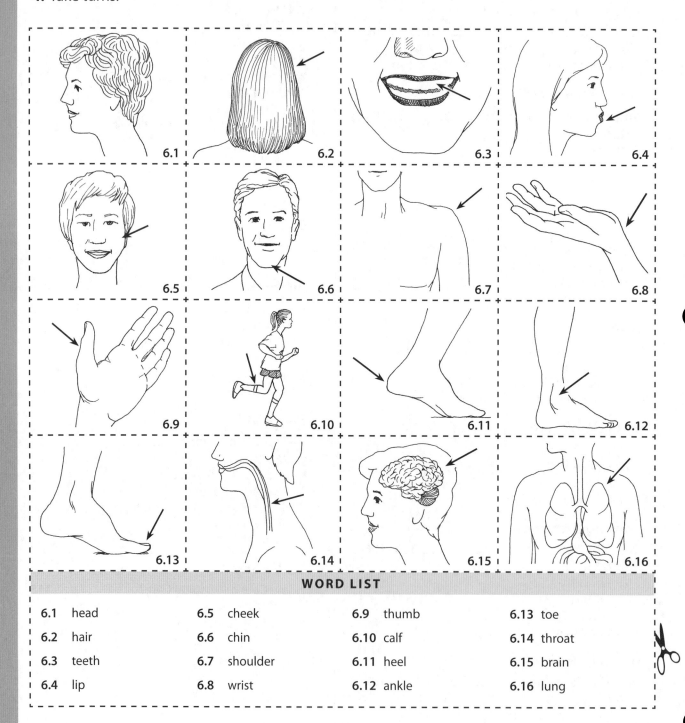

WORD LIST			
6.1 head	**6.5** cheek	**6.9** thumb	**6.13** toe
6.2 hair	**6.6** chin	**6.10** calf	**6.14** throat
6.3 teeth	**6.7** shoulder	**6.11** heel	**6.15** brain
6.4 lip	**6.8** wrist	**6.12** ankle	**6.16** lung

At the Drugstore

1. Work with a partner. Cut apart the cards.

2. Write the Word List words on the back of the cards.

3. Student A: Show the picture to your partner.
   Student B: Say the word or phrase.

4. Take turns.

WORD LIST

6.17 soap	**6.21** deodorant	**6.25** nail polish	**6.29** brush
6.18 shampoo	**6.22** toothpaste	**6.26** blow dryer	**6.30** nail clipper
6.19 body lotion	**6.23** perfume	**6.27** hair spray	**6.31** electric shaver
6.20 shaving cream	**6.24** lipstick	**6.28** comb	**6.32** razor

Health

What do you use it for?

1. Work with 3 classmates. Cut apart the cards. Put them face down in a pile.
2. Student A: Pick a card. Describe the word or phrase on the card.
   Students B, C, and D: Guess the word or phrase.
3. The first student to guess correctly keeps the card.
4. Take turns.

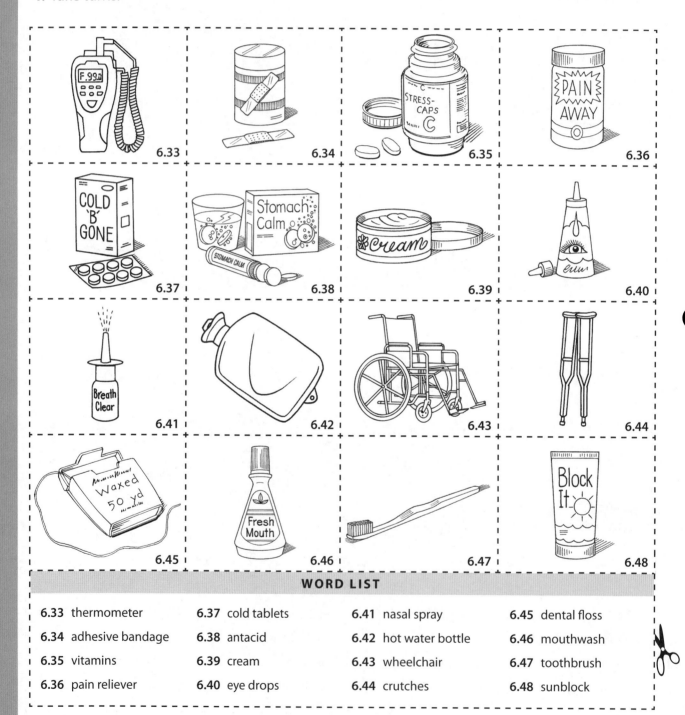

WORD LIST			
6.33 thermometer	**6.37** cold tablets	**6.41** nasal spray	**6.45** dental floss
6.34 adhesive bandage	**6.38** antacid	**6.42** hot water bottle	**6.46** mouthwash
6.35 vitamins	**6.39** cream	**6.43** wheelchair	**6.47** toothbrush
6.36 pain reliever	**6.40** eye drops	**6.44** crutches	**6.48** sunblock

Health and Personal Hygiene

1. Work with 3 classmates. Cut apart the cards. Put the cards face down in a pile.
2. Student A: Pick a card. Silently act out the action.
   Student B: Ask *What did he / she do?*
   Students C and D: Answer the question using the past tense. (*She brushed her teeth.*)
   Student B: Write what your classmates say.
3. Take turns.

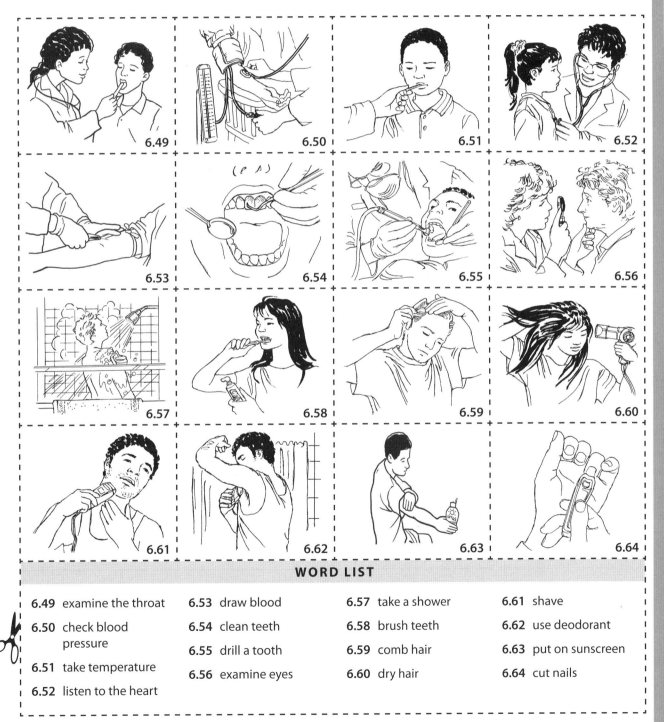

WORD LIST			
6.49 examine the throat	**6.53** draw blood	**6.57** take a shower	**6.61** shave
6.50 check blood pressure	**6.54** clean teeth	**6.58** brush teeth	**6.62** use deodorant
6.51 take temperature	**6.55** drill a tooth	**6.59** comb hair	**6.63** put on sunscreen
6.52 listen to the heart	**6.56** examine eyes	**6.60** dry hair	**6.64** cut nails

What's the matter? Grid

1. Use this grid with the picture cards on page 103.
2. Student A: Put one picture on each square on the grid. Don't show your partner your grid.
   Use the picture and the square to tell your partner a sentence.
   (*Bill has a headache.*)
   Student B: Listen to your partner. Check what you heard.
   (*Did you say Bill has a headache?*)
   Put the picture on the correct square on the grid.
3. When the grids are full, compare them. If they are the same, change roles. If not, try again.

Bill	Naima	I	Thomas
Mr. Williams	Alan	Luis	Mrs. Chu
Ms. Diaz	Cindy	Laura	Hector
Marta	Miguel	Alonzo	You

What's the matter? Cards

1. Use these picture cards with the grid on page 102.

2. Work with a partner. Cut apart the cards.

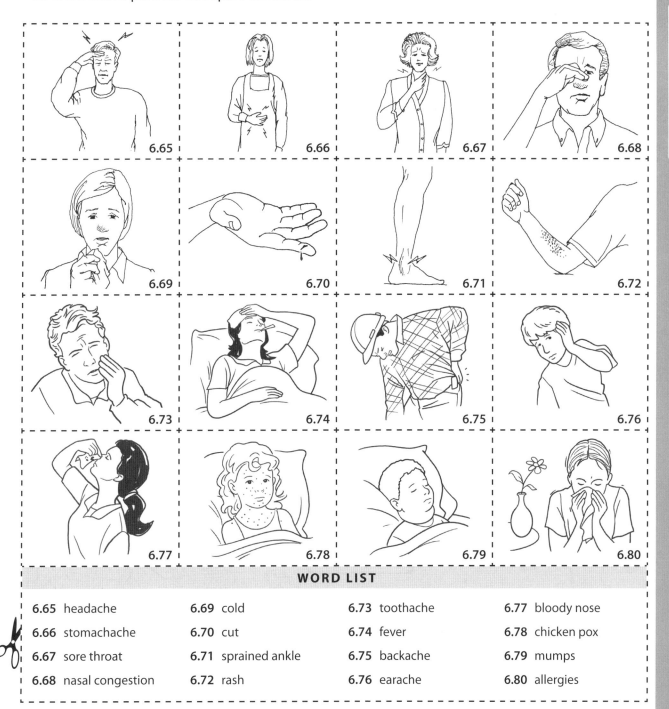

WORD LIST

6.65 headache	**6.69** cold	**6.73** toothache	**6.77** bloody nose
6.66 stomachache	**6.70** cut	**6.74** fever	**6.78** chicken pox
6.67 sore throat	**6.71** sprained ankle	**6.75** backache	**6.79** mumps
6.68 nasal congestion	**6.72** rash	**6.76** earache	**6.80** allergies

Health

GRAMMAR ACTIVITY

Health

Body Language

1. Work with 2 classmates.
2. Label what you see in the picture. Take turns.
3. Check your spelling in the *OPD*.

hand

▶ **What's Next?** Continue working with your group. Take turns describing parts of the body without saying the name of the part. Your group will try to figure out the answer. *It's inside your mouth. It helps you talk.* (tongue)

I need this! A

1. Find a partner with page 106 (B). Don't show your partner this paper.
2. Describe Picture A to your partner. Your partner will draw what you say.
3. Answer your partner's questions.

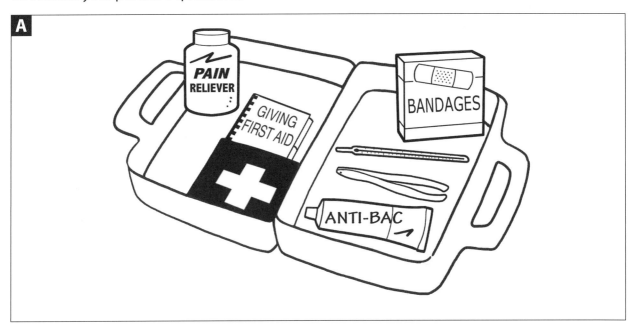

4. Listen to your partner describe Picture B. Draw what you hear. You can ask questions like these: *What's next to the _____? Is it large or small?*
5. When both pictures are complete, compare them.

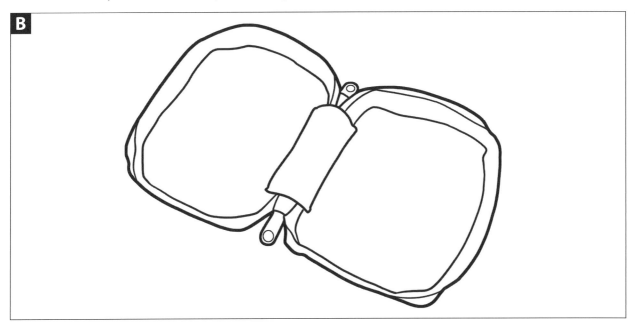

▶ **What's Next?** Work with a group. Which first aid supplies should everyone have? Make a list and share it with the class. Use everyone's information to make a class list.

I need this! B

1. Find a partner with page 105 (A). Don't show your partner this paper.
2. Listen to your partner describe Picture A. Draw what you hear. You can ask questions like these: *What's next to the _____? Is it large or small?*

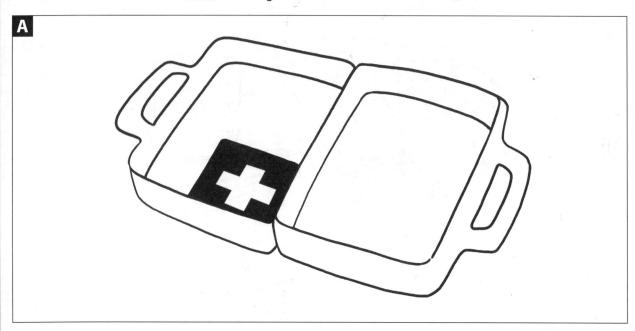

3. Describe Picture B to your partner. Your partner will draw what you say.
4. Answer your partner's questions.
5. When both pictures are complete, compare them.

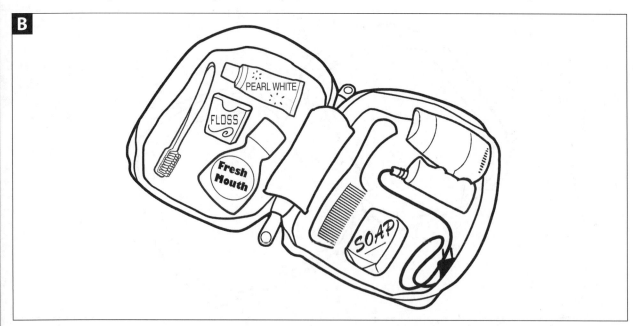

▶ **What's Next?** Work with a group. Which first aid supplies should everyone have? Make a list and share it with the class. Use everyone's information to make a class list.

What should I take?

1. Work with 3 or 4 classmates. Choose a Recorder.
2. Use the cards to make 10 different sentences or questions. The Recorder writes them down.

I	YOU	SHOULD	SHOULDN'T
TAKE	USE	WHAT	FOR
A	FEVER	COLD	CUT
BACKACHE	STOMACHACHE	BANDAGES	COLD TABLETS
ANTACIDS	PAIN RELIEVER	.	?

▶ **What's Next?** Share your sentences with the class. Which group made the most sentences? the most questions?

Health

A

Welby Community Clinic A

1. Find a partner with page 109 (B). Look at each other's picture.

2. Find 10 differences with your partner. Write the differences in the chart.

	A	B
1.	The receptionist is sitting.	The receptionist is standing.
2.		
3.		
4.		
5.		
6.		
7.		
8.		
9.		
10.		

▶ **What's Next?** Work with a group. Where can you go for health care? Where can you go in case of an emergency?

Health

Welby Community Clinic B

1. Find a partner with page 108 (A). Look at each other's picture.

2. Find 10 differences with your partner. Write the differences in the chart.

A	B
1. The receptionist is sitting.	The receptionist is standing.
2.	
3.	
4.	
5.	
6.	
7.	
8.	
9.	
10.	

▶ **What's Next?** Work with a group. Where can you go for health care? Where can you go in case of an emergency?

Health

GRAMMAR ACTIVITY

You're the doctor!

1. Read the questions. Mark your answers with a ✔.

2. Survey 5 classmates. Write their names, and mark their answers with a ✔.

Would you rather ...	My answers	_____ answers	_____ answers	_____ answers	_____ answers	_____ answers
wear glasses **OR** wear contact lenses?						
take throat lozenges **OR** take cough medicine?						
take cold tablets for a cold **OR** take vitamins for a cold?						
use a heating pad for a backache **OR** use an ice pack for a backache?						
use a nasal spray for nasal congestion **OR** use a humidifier for nasal congestion?						
get an injection **OR** take pills?						

3. Write sentences about each classmate you surveyed.

> Tom would rather wear contact lenses than glasses.

1. _____

2. _____

3. _____

4. _____

5. _____

4. Work with 2 classmates. Read your sentences out loud and compare them.

▶ **What's Next?** Write sentences about your answers.

Getting Ready

1. Work with 2 classmates.
2. Look at the picture. Read the first sentence. Think of more sentences to write about the picture.
3. Take turns writing sentences to continue the story.
4. Check your spelling in the *OPD*.

In the morning, Alan gets ready in his bathroom.

_____

_____

_____

_____

_____

_____

_____

_____

▶ **What's Next?** Continue working with your group. Write a paragraph about how you get ready for your day. Read your paragraph to your group.

What's happening at Wellnet? A

1. Find a partner with page 113 (B). Don't show your partner this paper.

2. Look at A. Ask your partner about the missing information in this class schedule. You can ask questions like these: *What time is the _____ class? Where is the _____ class? What do you learn in the _____ class?*

3. Write the missing information.

A

WELLNET COMMUNITY HEALTH EDUCATION SCHEDULE OF CLASSES

CLASS	DESCRIPTION	LOCATION	TIME
First Aid	CPR and rescue breathing	Brod Clinic _____	Session 1: 6/7 Session 2: 6/14 _____
Heimlich Maneuver	Emergency procedure for _____	Gold Clinic Room A-4	Session 1: _____ _____ PM
Lower Your _____	Make changes to diet and exercise	Nayo Clinic	6/9 _____ PM
Emergency Care	Techniques for drug overdose, _____, and _____	Children's Hospital West Wing Room 44	6/10: TBA _____ PM 6/24: 8–11 AM
Women and _____	Understanding breast cancer	Stein Clinic _____	One session: 7/16 6:30–9 PM

4. Look at B. Use this immunization schedule to answer your partner's questions.

5. When you are finished, compare your schedules with your partner's.

B

WELLNET LOW-COST IMMUNIZATION SCHEDULE

VACCINE	AGE	LOCATION	COST
Flu Vaccination	Seniors 55 and over	Shapiro Senior Center—Room 5	Free
Chicken pox	12–15 months 4–6 years	Children's Hospital Room B-3	$10.00
Measles, Mumps, & Rubella (MMR)	12–15 months 4–6 years	Children's Hospital Room A-9	$20.00
Tuberculosis (TB) Test	6 months and over	Wellnet Mobile Clinic	$5.00
Allergy Injection * MD authorized	Adults 21 and over	Nayo Clinic East Room 4	$25.00

▶ **What's Next?** Work with a partner. You are planning a health education class for your neighborhood. What classes would you offer? Make a brochure and share it with the class.

What's happening at Wellnet? B

1. Find a partner with page 112 (A). Don't show your partner this paper.
2. Look at A. Use this class schedule to answer your partner's questions.

A

WELLNET COMMUNITY HEALTH EDUCATION SCHEDULE OF CLASSES

CLASS	DESCRIPTION	LOCATION	TIME
First Aid	CPR and rescue breathing	Brod Clinic Room 12	Session 1: 6/7 Session 2: 6/14 9 AM–12 PM
Heimlich Maneuver	Emergency procedure for choking	Gold Clinic Room A-4	Session 1: 6/14 4–6 PM
Lower Your Blood Pressure	Make changes to diet and exercise	Nayo Clinic Auditorium A-1	6/9 7:30–9 PM
Emergency Care	Techniques for drug overdose, bleeding, and drowning	Children's Hospital/ West Wing Room 44	6/10: TBA 6/17: 5–8 PM 6/24: 8–11 AM
Women and Cancer	Understanding breast cancer	Stein Clinic Room 15	One session: 7/16 6:30–9 PM

3. Look at B. Ask your partner about the missing information in this immunization schedule. You can ask questions like these: *Where can you get a _____? How much is it?*
4. Write the missing information.
5. When you are finished, compare your schedules with your partner's.

B

WELLNET LOW-COST IMMUNIZATION SCHEDULE

VACCINE	AGE	LOCATION	COST
Flu Vaccination	Seniors 55 and over	Shapiro Senior Center— _____	Free
_____	12–15 months	Children's Hospital Room B-3	$10.00
Measles, _____, & Rubella (MMR)	4–6 years	Children's Hospital Room A-9	_____
Tuberculosis (TB) Test	_____	_____	_____
_____ Injection * MD authorized	Adults 21 and over	Nayo Clinic East	_____

▶ **What's Next?** Work with a partner. You are planning a health education class for your neighborhood. What classes would you offer? Make a brochure and share it with the class.

Please help me, Doctor!

1. Work with 2 classmates.
2. Write the character next to each line.
3. Choose your character. Write other lines you could say.
4. Practice saying the lines. Act out the role play.

The Scene
a patient at a doctor's office and at a pharmacy

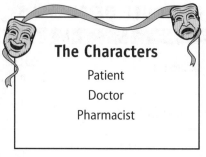

The Characters
Patient
Doctor
Pharmacist

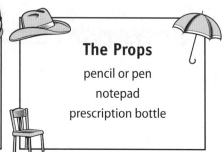

The Props
pencil or pen
notepad
prescription bottle

The Script

Doctor: How are you feeling?

_____ Not so good, Doctor. I'm coughing* a lot and my chest hurts.

_____ OK. How does your head feel?

_____ I think I had a fever this morning.

_____ I'll take your temperature, but I think you have the flu.

_____ Really?

_____ Yes, I'm going to give you a prescription. You can pick it up

at the pharmacy downstairs.

_____ Thank you, Doctor.

_____ Can I help you?

_____ Yes, I want to pick up a prescription. My name is _____.

_____ Let's see… Here you go. Make sure you take the pills with food.

_____ _____

_____ _____

_____ _____

*You can use other vocabulary for the underlined words.

▶ **What's Next?** Look at page 116 of the *OPD*. What should you do in these situations? Share your answers with the class. Your teacher will write your ideas on the board.

Home Care or Hospital Care?

1. Think about reasons to get health care at home or at the hospital.
2. Read the statements in the chart.
3. Write 2 more statements in the chart.
4. If the statement shows that home care is a good idea, ✔ that column. If the statement shows that hospital care is a good idea, ✔ that column.

Statements	home care	hospital care
Hospital staff can help you 24 hours a day, 7 days a week.		
At hospitals, patients usually have to share rooms.		
Hospitals can give you a translator.		
Most people don't sleep well in hospitals.		
Hospital meals are not very tasty.		
Health insurance doesn't often pay for home care.		
In the hospital, patients get emergency care right away.		
Sometimes elderly patients overdose on medicine by mistake.		
Family members can visit patients at any time.		
Many services, such as surgeries, are available only at the hospital.		

5. Work with a partner. Compare your ideas.
6. Write your and your partner's ideas.

I think that _____ is a good idea because _____

_____

My partner thinks that _____ is a good idea because _____

_____

► **What's Next?** Work as a class. How many students prefer home care? hospital care? Draw a bar graph on the board. Then discuss the results.

UNIT 7 | Community

People to Know

1. Work with a partner. Cut apart the cards.
2. Write the Word List words on the back of the cards.
3. Student A: Show the picture to your partner.
   Student B: Say the word or phrase.
4. Take turns.

WORD LIST

7.1	postal clerk	**7.5**	account manager	**7.9**	library clerk	**7.13**	firefighter
7.2	letter carrier	**7.6**	customer	**7.10**	Marine	**7.14**	mayor
7.3	security guard	**7.7**	street vendor	**7.11**	Coast Guard	**7.15**	governor
7.4	teller	**7.8**	pedestrian	**7.12**	National Guard	**7.16**	president

Crime and Punishment

1. Work with a partner. Cut apart the cards.
2. Write the Word List words on the back of the cards.
3. Student A: Show the picture to your partner.
   Student B: Say the word or phrase.
4. Take turns.

WORD LIST

7.17 burglary	7.21 drunk driving	7.25 vandalism	7.29 prisoner
7.18 arson	7.22 mugging	7.26 attorney	7.30 handcuffs
7.19 shoplifting	7.23 gang violence	7.27 judge	7.31 gun
7.20 illegal drugs	7.24 murder	7.28 jury	7.32 police officer

If you want to _____, you need this

1. Work with 3 classmates. Cut apart the cards. Put them face down in a pile.
2. Student A: Pick a card. Describe the word or phrase on the card.
    Students B, C, and D: Guess the word or phrase.
3. The first student to guess correctly keeps the card.
4. Take turns.

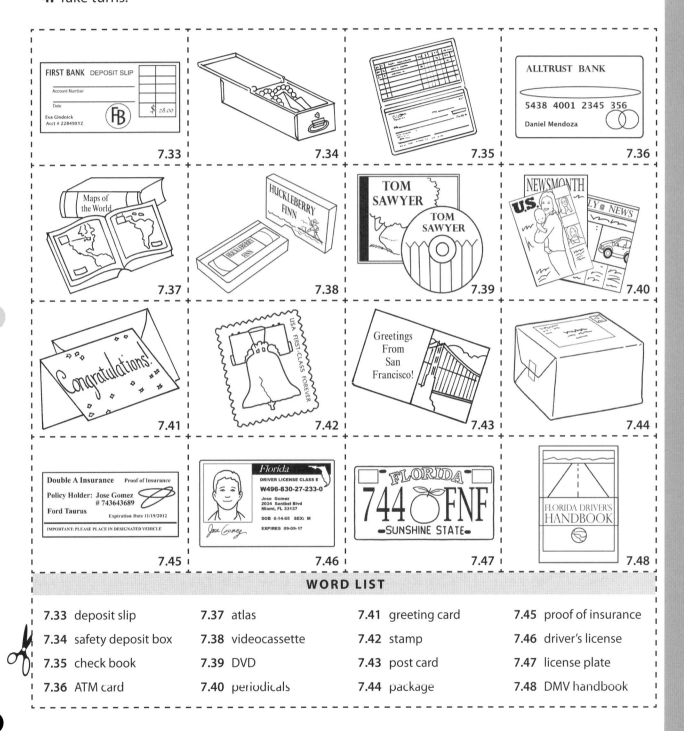

WORD LIST

7.33 deposit slip	7.37 atlas	7.41 greeting card	7.45 proof of insurance
7.34 safety deposit box	7.38 videocassette	7.42 stamp	7.46 driver's license
7.35 check book	7.39 DVD	7.43 post card	7.47 license plate
7.36 ATM card	7.40 periodicals	7.44 package	7.48 DMV handbook

Community

GRAMMAR ACTIVITY

Community Verbs

1. Work with 3 classmates. Cut apart the cards. Put the cards face down in a pile.
2. Student A: Pick a card. Silently act out the action.
   Student B: Ask *What is he / she doing?*
   Students C and D: Answer the question using the present continuous. (*She is crossing a street.*)
   Student B: Write what your classmates say.
3. Take turns.

WORD LIST

7.49 cross a street	**7.53** give a speech	**7.57** mail a card	**7.61** take cover
7.50 ride a bike	**7.54** applaud	**7.58** read a card	**7.62** lock the door
7.51 walk the dog	**7.55** write a card	**7.59** enter your pin number	**7.63** arrest a suspect
7.52 park the car	**7.56** put on a stamp	**7.60** withdraw cash	**7.64** convict a defendant

A Street Map Grid

1. Use this grid with the picture cards on page 122.
2. Student A: Put one picture on each square on the grid. Don't show your partner your grid.
   Use the picture and the square to tell your partner a sentence.
   (*The school is on First Street.*)
   Student B: Listen to your partner. Check what you heard.
   (*Did you say the school is on First Street?*)
   Put the picture on the correct square on the grid.
3. When the grids are full, compare them. If they are the same, change roles. If not, try again.

on First Street	on Second Street	on Third Street	on Fourth Street
on Avenue A	on Avenue B	on Avenue C	on Avenue D
on Oak Street	on Elm Street	on Maple Street	on Pine Street
on Main Street	on Grand Avenue	on Park Avenue	on Green Street

Community

GRAMMAR ACTIVITY

A Street Map Cards

1. Use these picture cards with the grid on page 121.

2. Work with a partner. Cut apart the cards.

Central High 7.65	Paradise Cinema 7.66	Brod Medical Center 7.67	UNITED ST 7.68
BOOK DROP 7.69	WESTERN BANK ATM 7.70	Hall of Justice 7.71	NYPD #44 7.72
ENGINE UNIT #4 7.73	RAY'S FOODTOWN VALENCIA ORANGES .79¢ lb. 7.74	Rx - Prescriptions 7.75	WELCOME TRADE SHOW 7.76
HAIRCUTS 7.77	7.78	GYM 7.79	EXIT ENTRANCE 7.80

WORD LIST

7.65 school	**7.69** library	**7.73** fire station	**7.77** barbershop
7.66 movie theater	**7.70** bank	**7.74** supermarket	**7.78** factory
7.67 hospital	**7.71** courthouse	**7.75** pharmacy	**7.79** gym
7.68 post office	**7.72** police station	**7.76** convention center	**7.80** parking garage

Around the Corner

1. Work with 2 classmates.
2. Label what you see in the picture. Take turns.
3. Check your spelling in the *OPD*.

magazine

▶ **What's Next?** What's in your favorite city? Draw a picture and label the places in your city. Talk about your picture with the class.

My Town A

1. Find a partner with page 125 (B). Don't show your partner this paper.

2. Describe Picture A to your partner. Your partner will write what you say.

3. Answer your partner's questions.

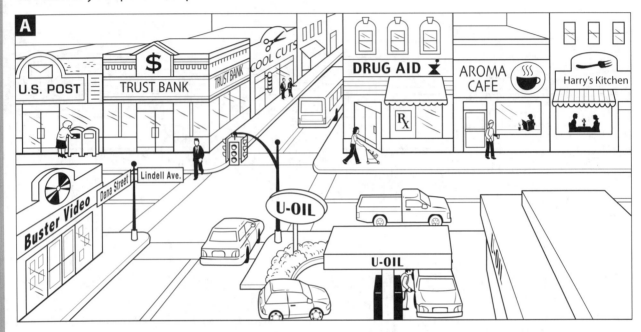

4. Listen to your partner describe Picture B. Write what you hear. You can ask questions like these: *Where did you say the _____ was? What's next to the _____?*

5. When both pictures are complete, compare them.

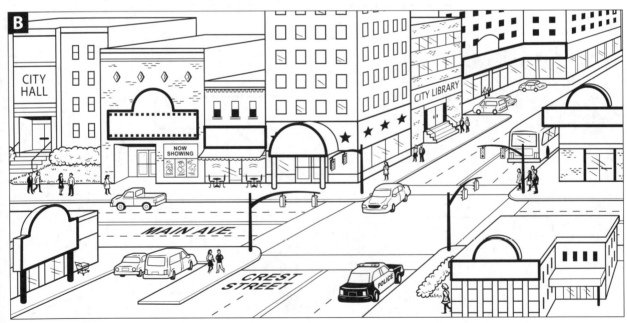

▶ **What's Next?** Work with a group to draw a map of the streets around your school. Include street names and other buildings. Keep copies of the new map to give to friends who want to learn English!

My Town B

1. Find a partner with page 124 (A). Don't show your partner this paper.
2. Listen to your partner describe Picture A. Write what you hear. You can ask questions like these: *Where did you say the _____ was? What's next to the _____?*

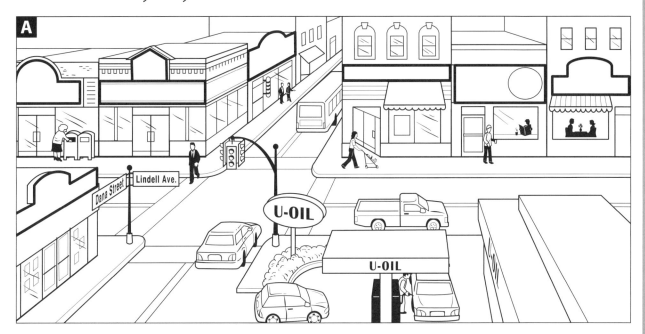

3. Describe Picture B to your partner. Your partner will write what you say.
4. Answer your partner's questions.
5. When both pictures are complete, compare them.

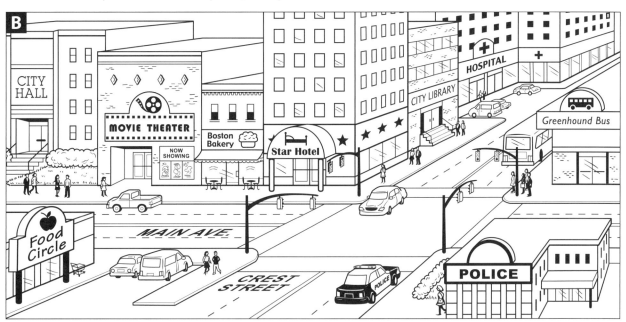

▶ **What's Next?** Work with a group to draw a map of the streets around your school. Include street names and other buildings. Keep copies of the new map to give to friends who want to learn English!

Community

GRAMMAR ACTIVITY

I'm lost!

1. Work with 3 or 4 classmates. Choose a Recorder.

2. Use the cards to make 10 different sentences or questions. The Recorder writes them down.

WHERE	IS	THE	BANK
LIBRARY	HOSPITAL	OFFICE	POST
BUILDING	NOT	ON	MAIN
ELM	STREET	NEAR	BEHIND
A	THERE	.	?

▶ **What's Next?** Share your sentences with the class. Which group made the most sentences? the most questions?

Paradise Hills Mall A

1. Find a partner with page 128 (B). Look at each other's picture.
2. Find 10 differences with your partner. Write the differences in the chart.

A	B
1. The music store is on the 1st floor.	The music store is on the 2nd floor.
2.	
3.	
4.	
5.	
6.	
7.	
8.	
9.	
10.	

▶ **What's Next?** Work with a partner. Think of a mall you go to. Tell your partner the types of stores it has and the names of the stores.

Community

A

Paradise Hills Mall B

1. Find a partner with page 127 (A). Look at each other's picture.

2. Find 10 differences with your partner. Write the differences in the chart.

A	B
1. The music store is on the 1st floor.	The music store is on the 2nd floor.
2.	
3.	
4.	
5.	
6.	
7.	
8.	
9.	
10.	

▶ **What's Next?** Work with a partner. Think of a mall you go to. Tell your partner the types of stores it has and the names of the stores.

How would you serve your country?

1. Read the questions. Mark your answers with a ✔.

2. Survey 5 classmates. Write their names, and mark their answers with a ✔.

Would you rather be ...	My answers	_____ answers	_____ answers	_____ answers	_____ answers	_____ answers
the president **OR** the vice-president?						
in the Senate **OR** in the House of Representatives?						
in the Army **OR** in the Navy?						
a governor **OR** a mayor?						
a justice **OR** on a jury?						
a prosecuting attorney **OR** a defense attorney?						

3. Write sentences about each classmate you surveyed.

Jenny would rather be the president than the vice-president.

1. _____

2. _____

3. _____

4. _____

5. _____

4. Work with 2 classmates. Read your sentences out loud and compare them.

▶ **What's Next?** Write sentences about your answers.

Community

GRAMMAR ACTIVITY

Community

Getting a Driver's License

1. Work with 2 classmates.
2. Look at the pictures. Read the first sentence. Think of more sentences to write about the pictures.
3. Take turns writing sentences to continue the story.
4. Check your spelling in the *OPD*.

Maria got her driver's license last month.

_____

_____

_____

_____

_____

_____

_____

_____

_____

▶ **What's Next?** What are other steps for getting a driver's license? Look at pages 136–137 of the *OPD*. Write more sentences.

Worldwide Disasters A

1. Find a partner with page 132 (B). Don't show your partner this paper.
2. Look at A. Ask your partner about the missing information in these headlines. You can ask questions like these: *When was the ____? Where was the ____? What happened in ____?*
3. Write the missing information.

4. Look at B. Use these headlines to answer your partner's questions.
5. When you are finished, compare your headlines with your partner's.

▶ **What's Next?** Continue working with your partner. Choose one of the disasters. Make a disaster kit for it. What would you put in your disaster kit?

▶ **Information Exchange B** (See page xxiii for Teacher's Notes.)

OPD pages 144–145

Community

Worldwide Disasters B

1. Find a partner with page 131 (A). Don't show your partner this paper.

2. Look at A. Use these headlines to answer your partner's questions.

A

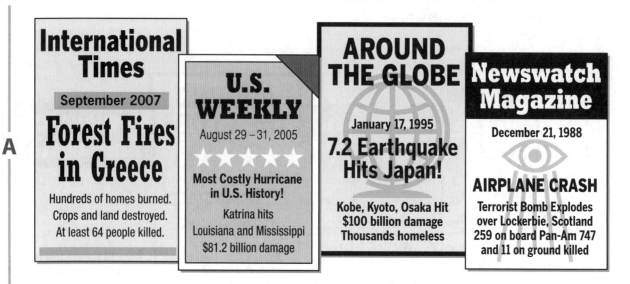

3. Look at B. Ask your partner about the missing information in these headlines. You can ask questions like these: *When was the _____? Where was the _____? What happened in _____?*

4. Write the missing information.

5. When you are finished, compare your headlines with your partner's.

B

▶ **What's Next?** Continue working with your partner. Choose one of the disasters. Make a disaster kit for it. What would you put in your disaster kit?

Order in the Court!

1. Work with 3 classmates.
2. Write the character next to each line.
3. Choose your character. Write other lines you could say.
4. Practice saying the lines. Act out the role play.

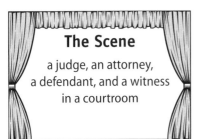

The Scene

a judge, an attorney, a defendant, and a witness in a courtroom

The Characters

Judge
Attorney
Defendant
Witness

The Props

pens
legal pads

The Script

Judge:	Please state your name for the court.
_____	My name is _____.
_____	Will the prosecuting attorney come forward?
_____	Where were you on the night of September 15?*
_____	I was working at the library. I worked until 10 p.m.
_____	Your honor, we call this man as a witness. Do you remember this woman?
_____	Yes, I saw her steal money from the bank.
_____	Do you remember what she was wearing?
_____	She was wearing black pants and a baseball cap.
_____	I can prove I'm innocent! Ask my manager!
_____	If you are guilty, the sentence is 5 months in jail.
_____	_____
_____	_____
_____	_____

* You can use other vocabulary for the underlined words.

▶ **What's Next?** Have one group come to the front of the class and present their trial. Then, as "jury members," discuss the case and decide on a verdict.

Community

Community

Traffic Cameras—Yes or No?

1. Think about reasons that the police have traffic cameras at intersections.
2. Read the statements in the chart.
3. Write 2 more statements in the chart.
4. If the statement shows that traffic cameras are a good idea, ✔ that column. If the statement shows that traffic cameras are a bad idea, ✔ that column.

Statements	good idea	bad idea
Traffic cameras will catch speeding drivers.		
Traffic cameras will catch people who don't stop at red lights.		
Traffic cameras may take pictures of innocent drivers by mistake.		
Traffic cameras are very expensive.		
Traffic cameras will make crossing the street safer for children and older people.		
People will get expensive traffic tickets.		
The police will have time to fight more dangerous crimes.		
Dangerous drivers will avoid streets with traffic cameras and drive on other streets.		
Pictures from traffic cameras will be difficult to fight in court.		
Traffic cameras will affect our privacy.		

5. Work with a partner. Compare your ideas.
6. Write your and your partner's ideas.

I think that installing traffic cameras is a _____ idea because _____

_____

My partner thinks that installing traffic cameras is a _____ idea because

_____

▶ **What's Next?** Take a stand. Your teacher will tell you where to stand if you think traffic cameras are a good idea and where to stand if you think traffic cameras are a bad idea.

Transportation

Vehicles

1. Work with a partner. Cut apart the cards.
2. Write the Word List words on the back of the cards.
3. Student A: Show the picture to your partner.
   Student B: Say the word or phrase.
4. Take turns.

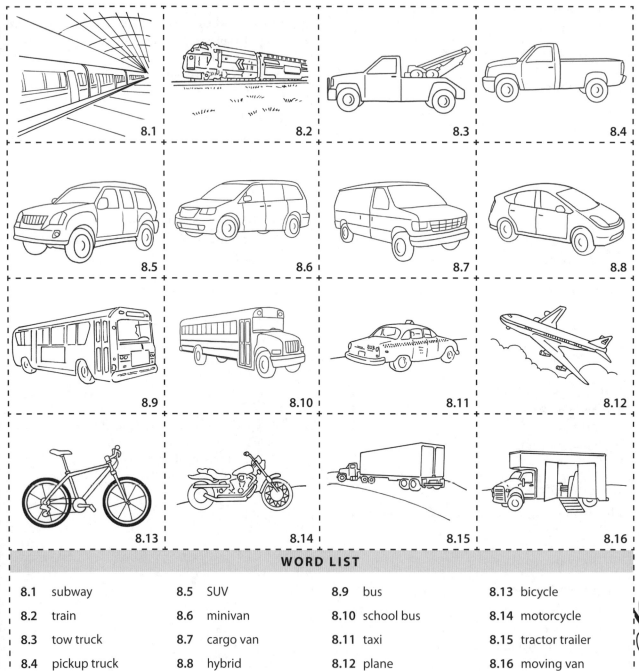

WORD LIST

8.1 subway	8.5 SUV	8.9 bus	8.13 bicycle
8.2 train	8.6 minivan	8.10 school bus	8.14 motorcycle
8.3 tow truck	8.7 cargo van	8.11 taxi	8.15 tractor trailer
8.4 pickup truck	8.8 hybrid	8.12 plane	8.16 moving van

Getting Around Town

1. Work with a partner. Cut apart the cards.
2. Write the Word List words on the back of the cards.
3. Student A: Show the picture to your partner.
   Student B: Say the word or phrase.
4. Take turns.

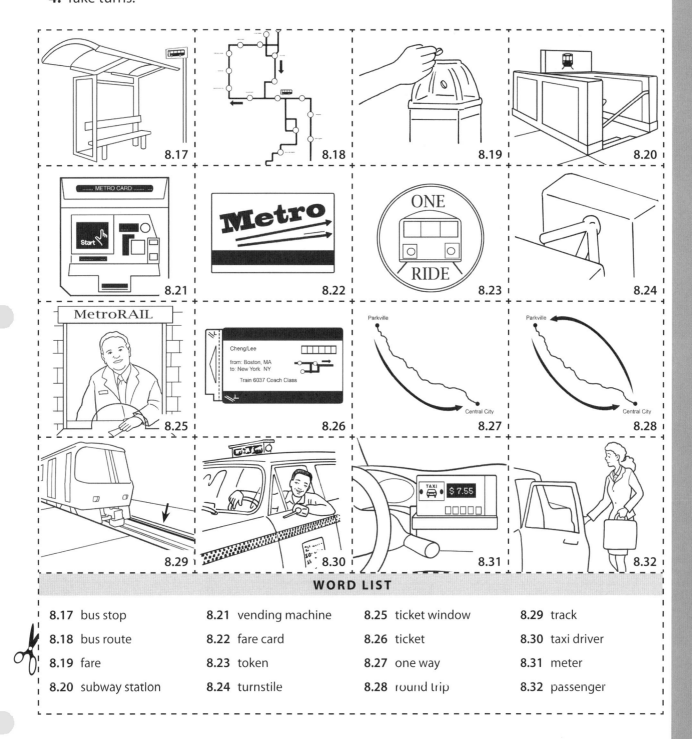

WORD LIST

8.17 bus stop	**8.21** vending machine	**8.25** ticket window	**8.29** track
8.18 bus route	**8.22** fare card	**8.26** ticket	**8.30** taxi driver
8.19 fare	**8.23** token	**8.27** one way	**8.31** meter
8.20 subway station	**8.24** turnstile	**8.28** round trip	**8.32** passenger

Transportation

Transportation

Traffic Signs

1. Work with 3 classmates. Cut apart the cards. Put them face down in a pile.
2. Student A: Pick a card. Describe the word or phrase on the card.
   Students B, C, and D: Guess the word or phrase.
3. The first student to guess correctly keeps the card.
4. Take turns.

WORD LIST

8.33 stop sign	8.37 U-turn OK sign	8.41 railroad crossing sign	8.45 yield sign
8.34 do not enter sign	8.38 dead end sign	8.42 no parking sign	8.46 merge sign
8.35 speed limit sign	8.39 right turn only sign	8.43 school crossing sign	8.47 no left turn sign
8.36 one way sign	8.40 pedestrian crossing sign	8.44 handicapped parking sign	8.48 road work sign

Move it!

1. Work with 3 classmates. Cut apart the cards. Put the cards face down in a pile.
2. Student A: Pick a card. Silently act out the action.
   Student B: Ask *What did he / she do?*
   Students C and D: Answer the question using the past tense. (*He went straight.*)
   Student B: Write what your classmates say.
3. Take turns.

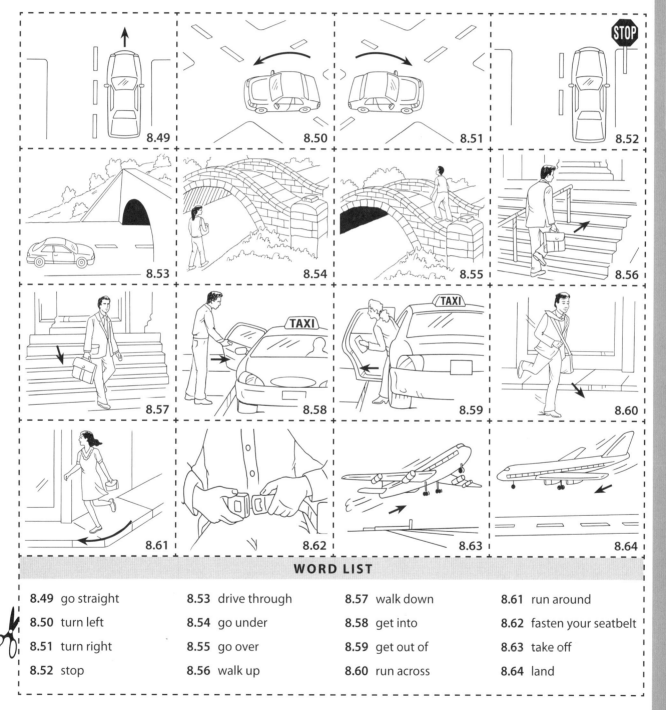

WORD LIST			
8.49 go straight	**8.53** drive through	**8.57** walk down	**8.61** run around
8.50 turn left	**8.54** go under	**8.58** get into	**8.62** fasten your seatbelt
8.51 turn right	**8.55** go over	**8.59** get out of	**8.63** take off
8.52 stop	**8.56** walk up	**8.60** run across	**8.64** land

Transportation

GRAMMAR ACTIVITY

Auto Repairs Grid

1. Use this grid with the picture cards on page 141.

2. Student A: Put one picture on each square on the grid. Don't show your partner your grid.

       Use the picture and the square to tell your partner a sentence.

       (*The horn of the sports car is broken.*)

    Student B: Listen to your partner. Check what you heard.

       (*Did you say the horn of the sports car is broken?*)

       Put the picture on the correct square on the grid.

3. When the grids are full, compare them. If they are the same, change roles. If not, try again.

sports car	4-door car	2-door car	hybrid
convertible	station wagon	SUV	minivan
camper	RV	limo	tow truck
pickup truck	cargo van	moving van	school bus

Auto Repairs Cards

1. Use these picture cards with the grid on page 140.
2. Work with a partner. Cut apart the cards.

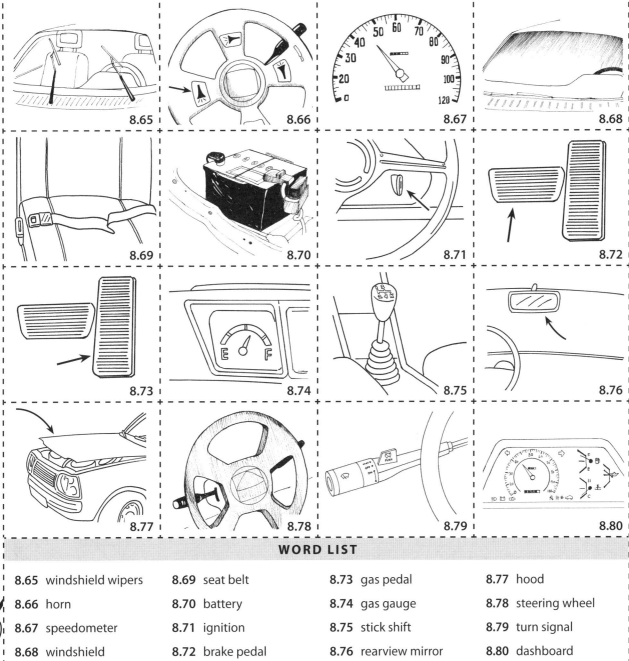

WORD LIST			
8.65 windshield wipers	**8.69** seat belt	**8.73** gas pedal	**8.77** hood
8.66 horn	**8.70** battery	**8.74** gas gauge	**8.78** steering wheel
8.67 speedometer	**8.71** ignition	**8.75** stick shift	**8.79** turn signal
8.68 windshield	**8.72** brake pedal	**8.76** rearview mirror	**8.80** dashboard

▶ **Round Table Label** (See page xvii for Teacher's Notes.)

OPD pages 150–151, 156

Transportation

Traveling on Route 66

1. Work with 2 classmates.
2. Label what you see in the picture. Take turns.
3. Check your spelling in the *OPD*.

▶ **What's Next?** Continue working with your group. What public transportation do you have in your area? Make a list and discuss each one. Use these questions: *How much is the fare? Is it fast? Is the schedule convenient? Where can you go?*

Check your map! A

1. Find a partner with page 144 (B). Don't show your partner this paper.

2. Describe Picture A to your partner. Your partner will draw what you say.

3. Answer your partner's questions.

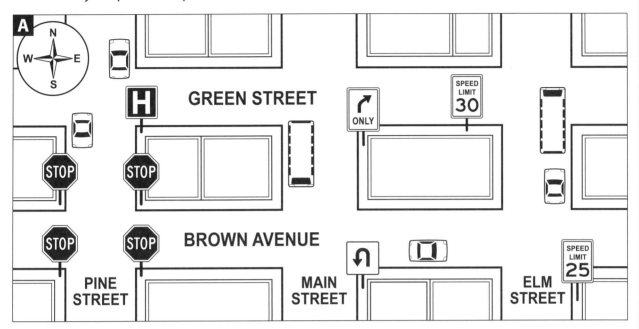

4. Listen to your partner describe Picture B. Draw what you hear. You can ask questions like these: *What signs are on _____ Street? Where is the _____ sign?*

5. When both pictures are complete, compare them.

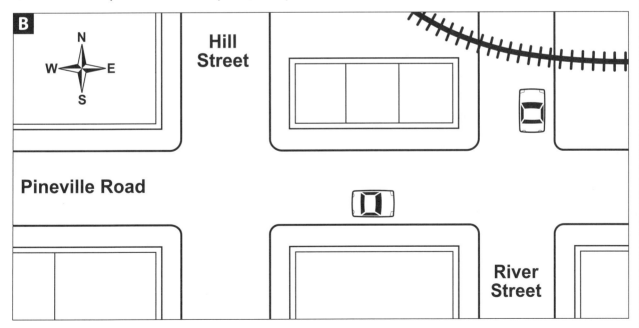

▶ **What's Next?** Work with a partner. Pick a location for yourself and a destination on Picture B. Ask your partner for directions to your destination. Take turns asking for and giving directions. Share your conversation with the class.

Transportation

Check your map! B

1. Find a partner with page 143 (A). Don't show your partner this paper.
2. Listen to your partner describe Picture A. Draw what you hear. You can ask questions like these: *What signs are on _____ Street? Where is the _____ sign?*

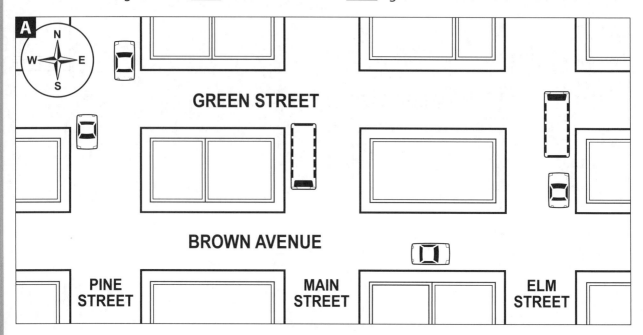

3. Describe Picture B to your partner. Your partner will draw what you say.
4. Answer your partner's questions.
5. When both pictures are complete, compare them.

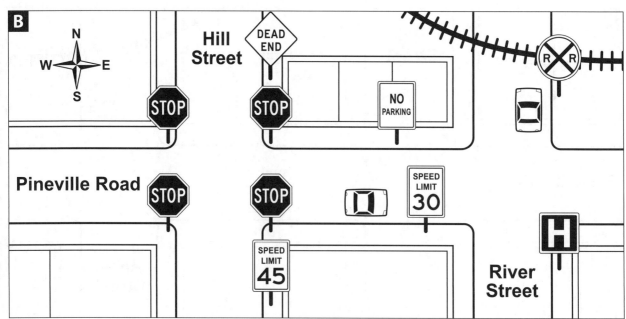

▶ **What's Next?** Work with a partner. Pick a location for yourself and a destination on Picture A. Ask your partner for directions to your destination. Take turns asking for and giving directions. Share your conversation with the class.

At the Mechanic

1. Work with 3 or 4 classmates. Choose a Recorder.
2. Use the cards to make 10 different sentences or questions. The Recorder writes them down.

THE	CAR	NEEDS	NEED
DOES	IT	A	NEW
BATTERY	TIRE	BUMPER	AIR CONDITIONER
HEADLIGHT	LICENSE PLATE	MORE	GAS
OIL	COOLANT	.	?

▶ **What's Next?** Share your sentences with the class. Which group made the most sentences? the most questions?

Transportation

A

Fly Skyair A

1. Find a partner with page 147 (B). Look at each other's picture.

2. Find 10 differences with your partner. Write the differences in the chart.

	A	B
1.	A computer is on the check-in counter.	There is no computer on the check-in counter.
2.		
3.		
4.		
5.		
6.		
7.		
8.		
9.		
10.		

▶ **What's Next?** Work with a partner. Look at the picture of the boarding area. Create a conversation between the ticket agent and the passenger. Share your conversation with the class.

Fly Skyair B

1. Find a partner with page 146 (A). Look at each other's picture.
2. Find 10 differences with your partner. Write the differences in the chart.

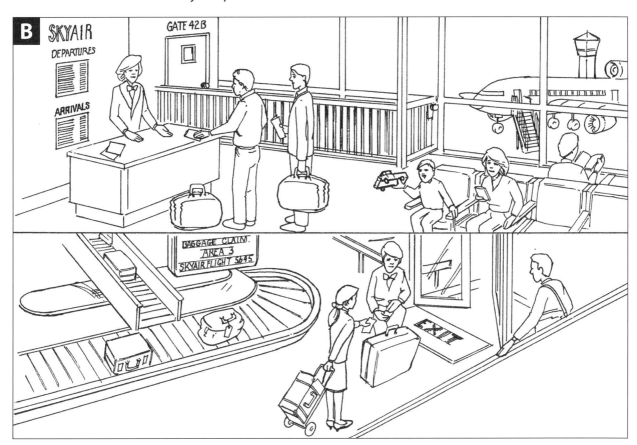

	A	B
1.	A computer is on the check-in counter.	There is no computer on the check-in counter.
2.		
3.		
4.		
5.		
6.		
7.		
8.		
9.		
10.		

▶ **What's Next?** Work with a partner. Look at the picture of the boarding area. Create a conversation between the ticket agent and the passenger. Share your conversation with the class.

Transportation

B

What's the best way to travel?

1. Read the questions. Mark your answers with a ✔.

2. Survey 5 classmates. Write their names, and mark their answer with a ✔.

Do you prefer to …	My answers	_____ answers	_____ answers	_____ answers	_____ answers	_____ answers
take a plane OR take a train?						
take a subway OR take a bus?						
take a taxi OR drive a car yourself?						
drive a pickup truck OR drive a sports car?						
use cash to pay your fare OR use a farecard to pay your fare?						
drive to school OR take public transportation to school?						

3. Write sentences about each classmate you surveyed.

Jorge prefers taking a plane to taking a train.

1. _____

2. _____

3. _____

4. _____

5. _____

4. Work with 2 classmates. Read your sentences out loud and compare them.

▶ **What's Next?** Write sentences about your answers.

A Day in the City

1. Work with 2 classmates.
2. Look at the pictures. Read the first sentence. Think of more sentences to write about the pictures.
3. Take turns writing sentences to continue the story.
4. Check your spelling in the *OPD*.

Last week Emily and Sophia spent a day in the city.

_____

_____

_____

_____

_____

_____

_____

_____

_____

▶ **What's Next?** Plan a field trip for your class. Decide where you can go, how you can get there, and what you can do. Share your plan with the class.

Transportation

Destination: San Francisco A

1. Find a partner with page 151 (B). Don't show your partner this paper.
2. Look at A. Ask your partner about the missing information in this travel schedule. You can ask questions like these: *What time does _____ leave? What's the fare for _____? How long does it take by _____?*
3. Write the missing information.

GLOBAL TRAVEL — DESTINATION SAN FRANCISCO!

Prepared for: S. Lanzano
TRAVEL OPTIONS, departing 8/15:

Air/Ground	Leave	Arrive	Travel Time	Fare
Skyair Nonstop Flight 244	New York City **8:30** AM	San Francisco	5 Hrs.	round trip
Skyair Direct Flight 1069	New York City	Chicago 1:00 PM		one way
Skyair Direct Flight 53	Chicago 2:00 PM	San Francisco		one way $265.00
Intertrak Railways Line	New York City	San Francisco	50 Hrs. (arrive 8/17)	round trip

4. Look at B. Use this sightseeing schedule to answer your partner's questions.
5. When you are finished, compare your schedules with your partner's.

GLOBAL TRAVEL — SEE SAN FRANCISCO!

SIGHTSEEING OPTIONS: **Prepared for: S. Lanzano**

TRANSPORTATION	LEAVE	PLACE	TIME	COST
Bay City Lines – Bus Tours				
Basic Tour Downtown	10 AM, 12 PM, 2 PM, 4 PM	Lincoln Park NW Corner	2 Hrs.	$29.00
Deluxe Tour Bay Area	9:30 AM, 2:30 PM	Union Square SE Corner	3 Hrs.	$45.00
Golden Gate Travel – Ride the Streetcar!				
City Tours	Every 30 Min.	Mason/Powell Line	45 Min.	$12.00
Downtown San Francisco	9 AM – 5 PM	Broadway/Van Ness Line		
Embarcadero Lines – See Alcatraz and San Francisco from the Bay!				
Ferry Tours – Red Line	8 AM, 11 AM, 2 AM	Pier 17	1 Hr.	$25.00
Blue Line	9 AM, 12 PM, 3 PM	Pier 15	1 1/2 Hrs.	$34.00

▶ **What's Next?** You are traveling to San Francisco. Which transportation will you choose for getting there? Which transportation will you choose for seeing the city? Think about cost, time, and convenience. Tell a partner about your choices.

Destination: San Francisco B

1. Find a partner with page 150 (A). Don't show your partner this paper.
2. Look at A. Use this travel schedule to answer your partner's questions.

GLOBAL TRAVEL — DESTINATION SAN FRANCISCO!

Prepared for: S. Lanzano
TRAVEL OPTIONS, departing 8/15:

Air/Ground	Leave	Arrive	Travel Time	Fare
Skyair Nonstop Flight 244	New York City 8:30 AM	San Francisco 10:30 AM	5 Hrs.	round trip $525.00
Skyair Direct Flight 1069	New York City 11:30 AM	Chicago 1:00 PM	2 1/2 Hrs.	one way $129.00
Skyair Direct Flight 53	Chicago 2:00 PM	San Francisco 4:30 PM	4 1/2 Hrs.	one way $265.00
Intertrak Railways Line	New York City 9:00 PM	San Francisco 12:00 AM	50 Hrs. (arrive 8/17)	round trip $398.00

3. Look at B. Ask your partner about the missing information in this sightseeing schedule. You can ask questions like these: *How much is the _____? How long is the _____?*
4. Write the missing information.
5. When you are finished, compare your schedules with your partner's.

GLOBAL TRAVEL — SEE SAN FRANCISCO!

SIGHTSEEING OPTIONS: **Prepared for: S. Lanzano**

TRANSPORTATION	LEAVE	PLACE	TIME	COST
Bay City Lines – Bus Tours				
Basic Tour Downtown	10 AM, 12 PM, 2 PM, 4 PM	Lincoln Park NW Corner	2 Hrs.	_____
Deluxe Tour Bay Area	9:30 AM, _____	Union Square SE Corner	_____	_____
Golden Gate Travel – Ride the Streetcar!				
City Tours	Every_____	Mason/Powell Line	45 Min.	_____
Downtown San Francisco	9 AM – 5 PM	Broadway/Van Ness Line		
Embarcadero Lines – See Alcatraz and San Francisco from the Bay!				
Ferry Tours – Red Line	8 AM, _____ , 2 AM	Pier 17	1 Hr.	_____
Blue Line	_____ ,12 PM, 3 PM	Pier _____	1 1/2 Hrs.	$34.00

▶ **What's Next?** You are traveling to San Francisco. Which transportation will you choose for getting there? Which transportation will you choose for seeing the city? Think about cost, time, and convenience. Tell a partner about your choices.

Transportation

Friendly Skies

1. Work with 2 classmates.
2. Write the character next to each line.
3. Choose your character. Write other lines you could say.
4. Practice saying the lines. Act out the role play.

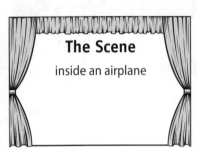

The Scene
inside an airplane

The Characters
Pilot
Flight attendant
Passenger

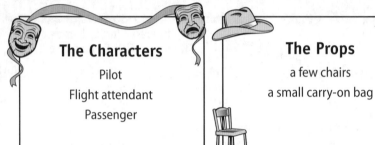

The Props
a few chairs
a small carry-on bag

The Script

Flight attendant:	Hello, welcome aboard. Please stow your bags in the overhead compartment.*
_____	Excuse me, could I change my seat?
_____	I'm sorry, but the flight is full.
_____	Oh, ok.
_____	Please don't forget to fasten your seatbelt.
_____	Good afternoon from the cockpit! This is Flight <u>2033</u> to <u>Dallas</u>.
_____	We hope you enjoy the flight.
_____	Is this plane really safe? I get so <u>nervous</u> when I fly!
_____	Yes, of course. It's safer than <u>a car</u>.
_____	Hello again, everyone. I'm sorry but our flight will be delayed because of <u>bad weather</u>.
_____	_____
_____	_____

*You can use other vocabulary for the underlined words.

▶ **What's Next?** Continue working with your group. Have you been on an airplane? How long was your longest flight? What was your experience like? If you haven't been on an airplane, do you want to fly in one? Discuss your answers with each other.

Drive a Car or Take Public Transportation?

1. Think about reasons to drive a car or to take public transportation.
2. Read the statements in the chart.
3. Write 2 more statements in the chart.
4. If the statement shows that driving a car is a good idea, ✔ that column. If the statement shows that taking public transportation is a good idea, ✔ that column.

Statements	driving a car	taking public transportation
You can travel at any time and to any place you want to go.		
Parking is a hard to find and can be expensive.		
Insurance, registration, maintenance, and gas are expensive.		
Trains and subways are often late.		
You have to walk to and from the stop or station.		
You have to wait for the bus in the cold and the rain.		
After work, it's easy to drive to the supermarket, bank, or school.		
Public transportation saves energy and makes less pollution.		
You can read or sleep on a train or a bus.		
SUVs and minivans are great for families.		

5. Work with a partner. Compare your ideas.
6. Write your and your partner's ideas.

I think that _____ is a good idea because

_____

My partner thinks that _____ is a good idea because

_____

▶ **What's Next?** Work as a class. How many students prefer driving a car? How many students prefer taking public transportation? Draw a bar graph on the board. Then discuss the results.

Work

Things Around the Workplace (Inside)

1. Work with a partner. Cut apart the cards.
2. Write the Word List words on the back of the cards.
3. Student A: Show the picture to your partner.
   Student B: Say the word or phrase.
4. Take turns.

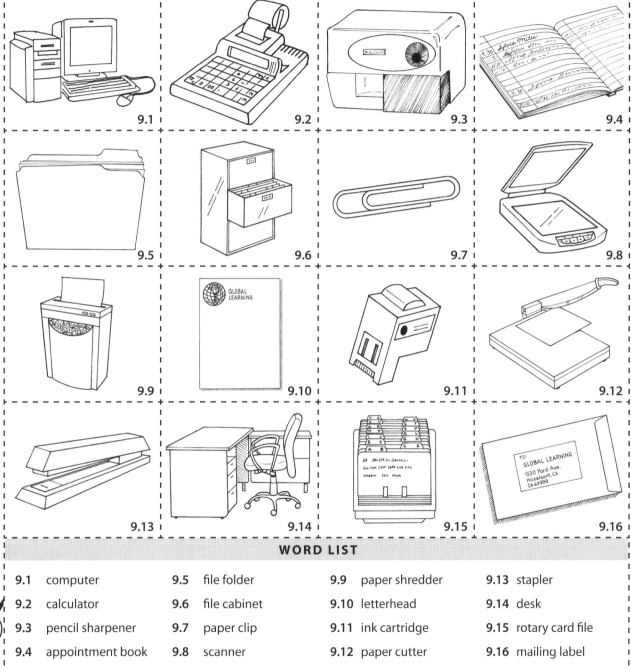

9.1 9.2 9.3 9.4
9.5 9.6 9.7 9.8
9.9 9.10 9.11 9.12
9.13 9.14 9.15 9.16

WORD LIST

9.1	computer	**9.5**	file folder	**9.9**	paper shredder	**9.13** stapler
9.2	calculator	**9.6**	file cabinet	**9.10**	letterhead	**9.14** desk
9.3	pencil sharpener	**9.7**	paper clip	**9.11**	ink cartridge	**9.15** rotary card file
9.4	appointment book	**9.8**	scanner	**9.12**	paper cutter	**9.16** mailing label

Things Around the Workplace (Outside)

1. Work with a partner. Cut apart the cards.
2. Write the Word List words on the back of the cards.
3. Student A: Show the picture to your partner.
   Student B: Say the word or phrase.
4. Take turns.

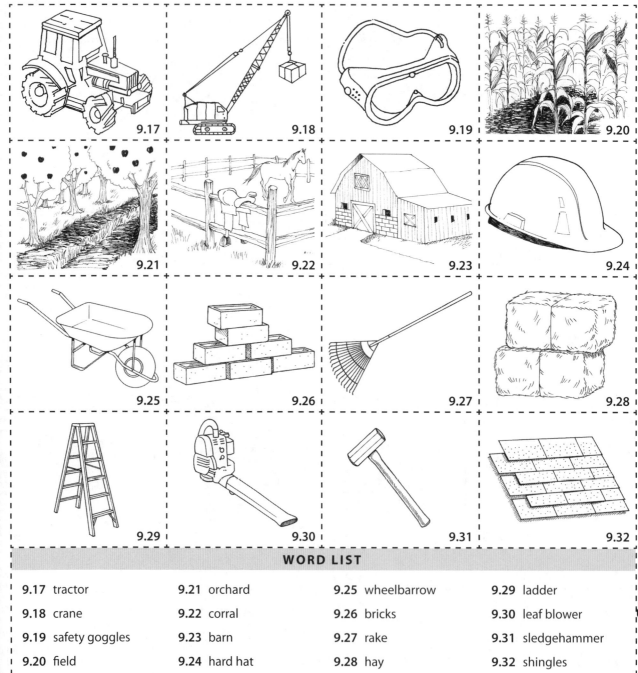

9.17
9.18
9.19
9.20
9.21
9.22
9.23
9.24
9.25
9.26
9.27
9.28
9.29
9.30
9.31
9.32

WORD LIST

9.17 tractor	**9.21** orchard	**9.25** wheelbarrow	**9.29** ladder
9.18 crane	**9.22** corral	**9.26** bricks	**9.30** leaf blower
9.19 safety goggles	**9.23** barn	**9.27** rake	**9.31** sledgehammer
9.20 field	**9.24** hard hat	**9.28** hay	**9.32** shingles

▶ **Guess What? Cards** (See page xiv for Teacher's Notes.)   *OPD* pages 180–181

Work

Tools and Building Supplies

1. Work with 3 classmates. Cut apart the cards. Put them face down in a pile.

2. Student A: Pick a card. Describe the word or phrase on the card.
Students B, C, and D: Guess the word or phrase.

3. The first student to guess correctly keeps the card.

4. Take turns.

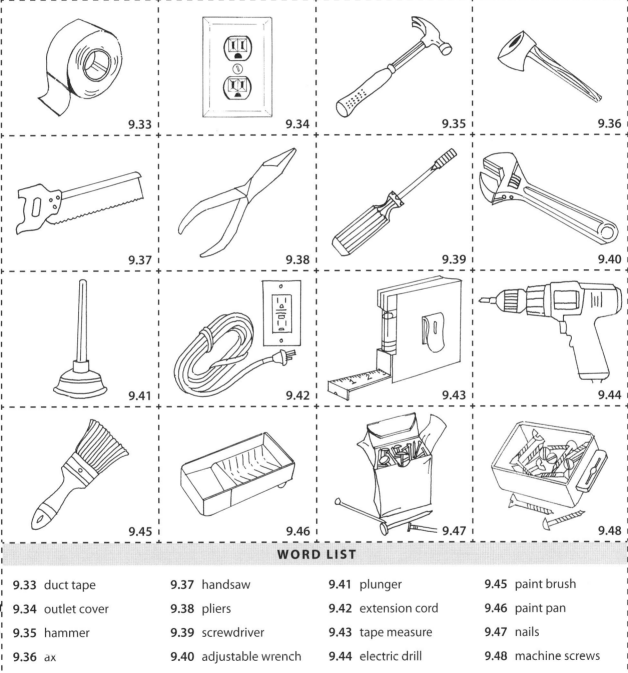

WORD LIST

9.33 duct tape	**9.37** handsaw	**9.41** plunger	**9.45** paint brush
9.34 outlet cover	**9.38** pliers	**9.42** extension cord	**9.46** paint pan
9.35 hammer	**9.39** screwdriver	**9.43** tape measure	**9.47** nails
9.36 ax	**9.40** adjustable wrench	**9.44** electric drill	**9.48** machine screws

What's happening at work today?

1. Work with 3 classmates. Cut apart the cards. Put the cards face down in a pile.

2. Student A: Pick a card. Silently act out the action.

Student B: Ask *What is he / she doing?*

Students C and D: Answer the question using the present continuous. (*She is faxing a document.*)

Student B: Write what your classmates say.

3. Take turns.

WORD LIST			
9.49 fax a document	**9.53** staple	**9.57** trim the hedges	**9.61** install a tile
9.50 make copies	**9.54** shake hands	**9.58** water the plants	**9.62** lay bricks
9.51 take a message	**9.55** mow the lawn	**9.59** plant a tree	**9.63** paint
9.52 type a letter	**9.56** rake the leaves	**9.60** hammer	**9.64** milk

What's his job? Grid

1. Use this grid with the picture cards on page 160.
2. Student A: Put one picture on each square on the grid. Don't show your partner your grid.
    Use the picture and the square to tell your partner a sentence.
    (*Jose is a farm worker.*)
   Student B: Listen to your partner. Check what you heard.
    (*Did you say Jose is a farm worker?*)
    Put the picture on the correct square on the grid.
3. When the grids are full, compare them. If they are the same, change roles. If not, try again.

Jose	Sharma	Patricia	Eduardo
Ms. Lee	Juanita	Mr. Sanchez	Ellen
Pablo	Michael	Sofia	Jenny
Kofi	Louisa	Glen	Mrs. Brown

What's his job? Cards

1. Use these picture cards with the grid on page 159.

2. Work with a partner. Cut apart the cards.

| 9.65 | 9.66 | 9.67 | 9.68 |

| 9.69 | 9.70 | 9.71 | 9.72 |

| 9.73 | 9.74 | 9.75 | 9.76 |

| 9.77 | 9.78 | 9.79 | 9.80 |

WORD LIST

9.65 farmworker	**9.69** welder	**9.73** mover	**9.77** garment worker
9.66 construction worker	**9.70** assembler	**9.74** gardener	**9.78** homemaker
9.67 computer software engineer	**9.71** carpenter	**9.75** server	**9.79** model
9.68 accountant	**9.72** painter	**9.76** business person	**9.80** factory worker

Work

GRAMMAR ACTIVITY

▶ **Round Table Label** (See page xvii for Teacher's Notes.)

OPD pages 182–183

Work

This office is a mess!

1. Work with 2 classmates.
2. Label what you see in the picture. Take turns.
3. Check your spelling in the *OPD*.

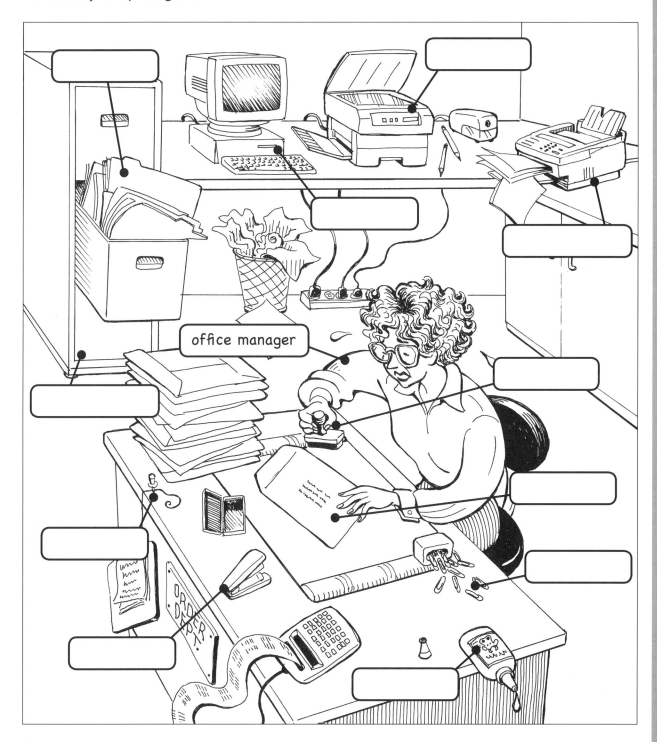

office manager

▶ **What's Next?** Work with a partner. You are an office manager for a big company. You have $100 for office supplies for a new employee. What do you buy? Tell your partner about the items you chose and why you chose them.

My Cubicle A

1. Find a partner with page 163 (B). Don't show your partner this paper.
2. Describe Picture A to your partner. Your partner will draw what you say.
3. Answer your partner's questions.

4. Listen to your partner describe Picture B. Draw what you hear. You can ask questions like these: *Where did you say the _____ was? How many _____ are there?*
5. When both pictures are complete, compare them.

▶ **What's Next?** Design your own cubicle. What items do you want and where do you want them on your desk? Draw a picture and show it to a classmate.

My Cubicle B

1. Find a partner with page 162 (A). Don't show your partner this paper.
2. Listen to your partner describe Picture A. Draw what you hear. You can ask questions like these: *Where did you say the _____ was? How many _____ are there?*

3. Describe Picture B to your partner. Your partner will draw what you say.
4. Answer your partner's questions.
5. When both pictures are complete, compare them.

▶ **What's Next?**　Design your own cubicle. What items do you want and where do you want them on your desk? Draw a picture and show it to a classmate.

Looking for a Job

1. Work with 3 or 4 classmates. Choose a Recorder.

2. Use the cards to make 10 different sentences or questions. The Recorder writes them down.

HE	SHE	I	YOU
WANT	WANTS	TO	BE
A	DOES	DO	CAN
NOT	REPORTER	NURSE	WRITER
CARPENTER	SERVER	.	?

▶ **What's Next?** Share your sentences with the class. Which group made the most sentences? The most questions?

On the Assembly Line A

1. Find a partner with page 166 (B). Look at each other's picture.
2. Find 10 differences with your partner. Write the differences in the chart.

A	B
1. The fire extinguisher is on the wall.	The fire extinguisher is on the floor.
2.	
3.	
4.	
5.	
6.	
7.	
8.	
9.	
10.	

▶ **What's Next?** Continue working with your partner. Decide which safety equipment you need in the following places: an office, a farm, a construction site, a hotel. Share your ideas with the class.

On the Assembly Line B

1. Find a partner with page 165 (A). Look at each other's picture.

2. Find 10 differences with your partner. Write the differences in the chart.

	A	**B**
1.	The fire extinguisher is on the wall.	The fire extinguisher is on the floor.
2.		
3.		
4.		
5.		
6.		
7.		
8.		
9.		
10.		

▶ **What's Next?** Continue working with your partner. Decide which safety equipment you need in the following places: an office, a farm, a construction site, a hotel. Share your ideas with the class.

I want that job!

1. Read the questions. Mark your answers with a ✔.

2. Survey 5 classmates. Write their names, and mark their answers with a ✔.

Would you rather …	My answers	____ answers	____ answers	____ answers	____ answers	____ answers
drive a truck **OR** operate heavy machinery?						
supervise adults **OR** take care of children?						
solve math problems **OR** speak another language?						
transcribe notes **OR** take dictation?						
scan a document **OR** fax a document?						
wait on customers **OR** use a cash register?						

3. Write sentences about each classmate you surveyed.

Eva would rather drive a truck.

1. _____

2. _____

3. _____

4. _____

5. _____

4. Work with 2 classmates. Read your sentences out loud and compare them.

▶ **What's Next?** Write sentences about your answers.

Work

What is Javier building?

1. Work with 2 classmates.
2. Look at the pictures. Read the first sentence. Think of more sentences to write about the pictures.
3. Take turns writing sentences to continue the story.
4. Check your spelling in the *OPD*.

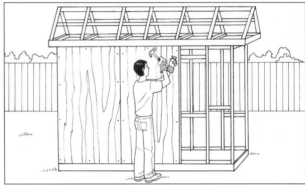

Javier likes to build things in his free time.

_____

_____

_____

_____

_____

_____

_____

_____

▶ **What's Next?** What do you want to build or make for your home? What tools and building supplies do you need? Tell a classmate about your project.

The Classifieds A

1. Find a partner with page 170 (B). Don't show your partner this paper.
2. Look at A. Ask your partner about the missing information in these classified ads. You can ask questions like these: *What experience do you need? What are the benefits? How do you apply?*
3. Write the missing information.

4. Look at B. Use these classified ads to answer your partner's questions.
5. When you are finished, compare your classified ads with your partner's.

▶ **What's Next?** Continue working with your partner. Choose one job from this page and practice a job interview. Decide who will be the interviewer and the applicant. Use these questions: *Tell me about your experience. Why are you interested in the job? Do you offer training?* Role play your interview for the class.

Work

The Classifieds B

1. Find a partner with page 169 (A). Don't show your partner this paper.

2. Look at A. Use these classified ads to answer your partner's questions.

A

3. Look at B. Ask your partner about the missing information in these classified ads. You can ask questions like these: *What experience do you need? What are the benefits? How do you apply?*

4. Write the missing information.

5. When you are finished, compare your classified ads with your partner's.

B

Daily ☀ News

EMPLOYMENT OPPORTUNITIES

ADMINISTRATIVE ASSISTANT	BABYSITTER	_____	SERVER
1 year experience Full time or part time Must be able to _____ and _____ Call (667) 555-3578; ask for Ms. Garcia	Excellent pay per hour Work on weekends Need to _____ and _____ of children **Call evenings:** **(314) 555-2205** ...bysitter for 4 adorable	*Loren Flower Shop* Need to _____ a truck Will provide _____ Come to store to _____ _____: 98 Third Ave. by Copley Station Deliver for Pizza Perfect	GINO'S DELI Looking for friendly staff Will need _____ and use a _____ _____ application and apply online: *www.ginosdeli.com*

▶ **What's Next?** Continue working with your partner. Choose one job from this page and practice a job interview. Decide who will be the interviewer and the applicant. Use these questions: *Tell me about your experience. Why are you interested in the job? Do you offer training?* Role play your interview for the class.

A Five-Star Hotel

1. Work with 3 classmates.
2. Write the character next to each line.
3. Choose your character. Write other lines you could say.
4. Practice saying the lines. Act out the role play.

The Scene
workers at a hotel are helping guests

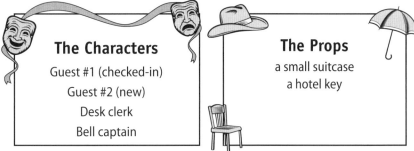

The Characters
Guest #1 (checked-in)

Guest #2 (new)

Desk clerk

Bell captain

The Props
a small suitcase
a hotel key

The Script

Guest #1: Could you help me? I lost a brown suitcase.* Can you check the luggage cart?

_____ Sure. I'll call the bell hop. He'll be here in 5 minutes.

_____ I also want to change rooms because the heater doesn't work.

_____ Oh, I'm sorry. The front desk can help you with that.

_____ Hello, welcome to Star Hotel. Do you have a reservation?

_____ Yes, I do. The name is Chan. Is it possible to stay one more night?

_____ Sure. So you'll check out on Tuesday?

_____ Yes, that'd be great.

_____ Here's the key for room 45. When you get off the elevator, turn right.

_____ Great! And you have a pool on the 5th floor?

_____ _____

_____ _____

_____ _____

_____ _____

*You can use other vocabulary for the underlined words.

▶ **What's Next?** Continue working with your group. You are opening a new hotel in your city. Where would it be? How big or small would it be? What services would you offer? How much would a room cost? Share your ideas with the class.

Work for Yourself or Someone Else?

1. Think about reasons to work for yourself or to work for someone else.
2. Read the statements in the chart.
3. Write 2 more statements in the chart.
4. If the statement shows that working for yourself is a good idea, ✔ that column. If the statement shows that working for someone else is a good idea, ✔ that column.

Statements	working for yourself	working for someone else
Many employers have online courses for new employees.		
Many companies give two weeks paid vacation.		
The government gives loans to people starting their own businesses.		
You can work with your family in your own business.		
Nobody can fire you if you are the boss.		
More experienced workers can give new employees on-the-job training.		
You have more job security if you work for someone else.		
Some jobs pay for cars, uniforms, and travel.		
In your own business, you can make your own schedule.		
You can do the work you like in your own business.		

5. Work with a partner. Compare your ideas.
6. Write your and your partner's ideas.

I think that working for _____ is a good idea because

_____

My partner thinks that working for _____ is a good idea because

_____

▶ **What's Next?** Take a stand. Your teacher will tell you where to stand if you think working for yourself is a good idea and where to stand if you think working for someone else is a good idea.

Lines and Shapes

1. Work with a partner. Cut apart the cards.
2. Write the Word List words on the back of the cards.
3. Student A: Show the picture to your partner.
   Student B: Say the word or phrase.
4. Take turns.

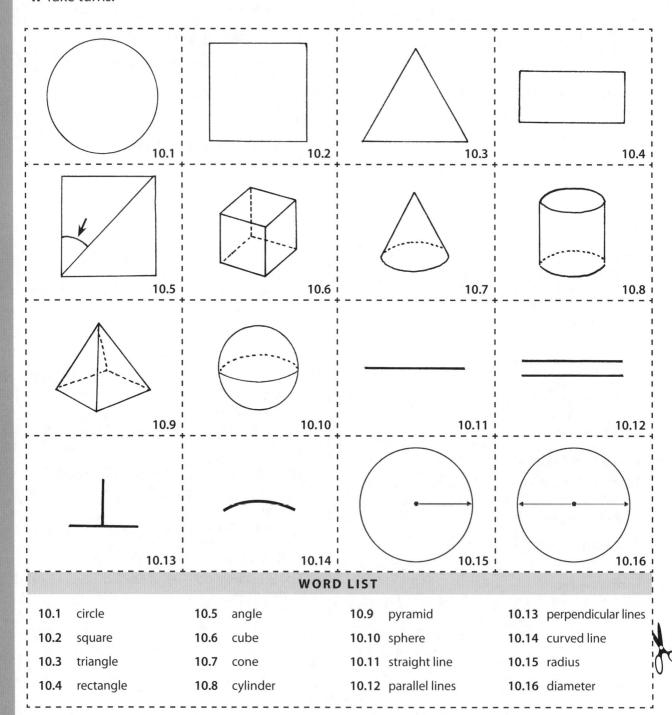

10.1	10.2	10.3	10.4
10.5	10.6	10.7	10.8
10.9	10.10	10.11	10.12
10.13	10.14	10.15	10.16

WORD LIST

10.1	circle	10.5	angle	10.9	pyramid	10.13	perpendicular lines
10.2	square	10.6	cube	10.10	sphere	10.14	curved line
10.3	triangle	10.7	cone	10.11	straight line	10.15	radius
10.4	rectangle	10.8	cylinder	10.12	parallel lines	10.16	diameter

Areas of Study

Computers

1. Work with a partner. Cut apart the cards.
2. Write the Word List words on the back of the cards.
3. Student A: Show the picture to your partner.
   Student B: Say the word or phrase.
4. Take turns.

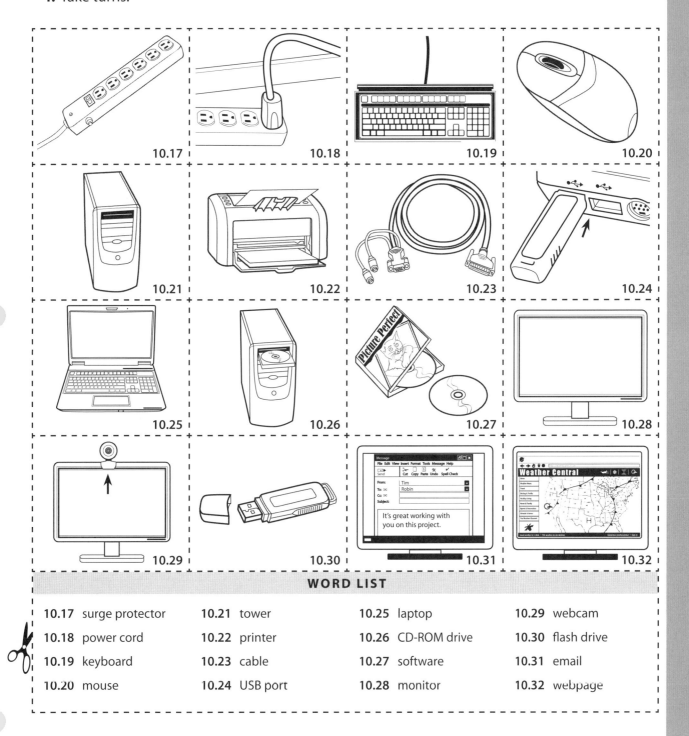

WORD LIST			
10.17 surge protector	**10.21** tower	**10.25** laptop	**10.29** webcam
10.18 power cord	**10.22** printer	**10.26** CD-ROM drive	**10.30** flash drive
10.19 keyboard	**10.23** cable	**10.27** software	**10.31** email
10.20 mouse	**10.24** USB port	**10.28** monitor	**10.32** webpage

Areas of Study

Areas of Study

At School

1. Work with 3 classmates. Cut apart the cards. Put them face down in a pile.
2. Student A: Pick a card. Describe the word or phrase on the card.
   Students B, C, and D: Guess the word or phrase.
3. The first student to guess correctly keeps the card.
4. Take turns.

WORD LIST

10.33 preschool	10.37 technical school	10.41 language arts	10.45 physical education
10.34 elementary school	10.38 community college	10.42 math	10.46 art
10.35 middle school	10.39 university	10.43 science	10.47 ESL
10.36 high school	10.40 adult school	10.44 history	10.48 music

I've been there

1. Work with 3 classmates. Cut apart the cards. Put them face down in a pile.
2. Student A: Pick a card. Describe the word or phrase on the card.
   Students B, C, and D: Guess the word or phrase.
3. The first student to guess correctly keeps the card.
4. Take turns.

WORD LIST

10.49 waterfall	**10.53** island	**10.57** shore	**10.61** valley
10.50 river	**10.54** beach	**10.58** mountain peak	**10.62** plains
10.51 desert	**10.55** forest	**10.59** mountain range	**10.63** meadow
10.52 peninsula	**10.56** lake	**10.60** hills	**10.64** pond

What are you taking? Grid

1. Use this grid with the picture cards on page 179.
2. Student A: Put one picture on each square on the grid. Don't show your partner your grid.
   Use the picture and the square to tell your partner a sentence.
   (*Mark is taking English composition.*)

   Student B: Listen to your partner. Check what you heard.
   (*Did you say Mark is taking English composition?*)
   Put the picture on the correct square on the grid.
3. When the grids are full, compare them. If they are the same, change roles. If not, try again.

Mark	Carlos	Ana and Maria	Tuyet
Felipe	Ms. Patel	Amelia	Wendy and May
Frank and Ray	Min	Sara	Paco
Jill	I	We	They

What are you taking? Cards

1. Use these picture cards with the grid on page 178.
2. Work with a partner. Cut apart the cards.

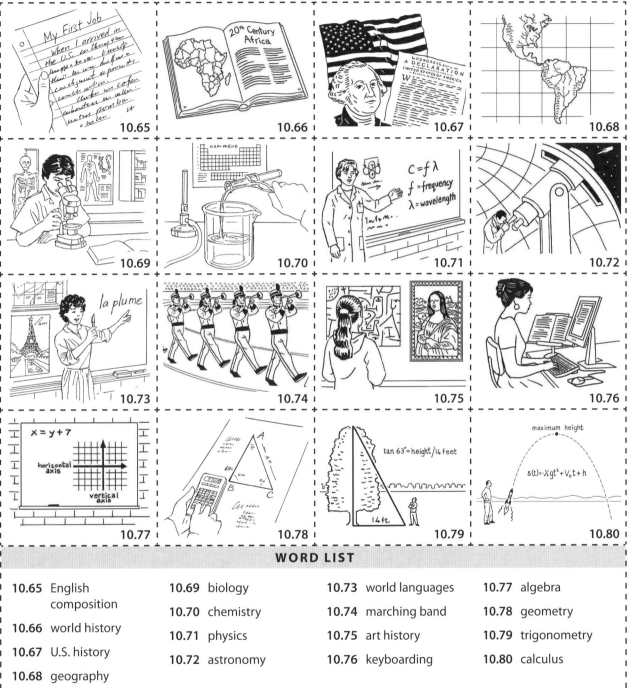

WORD LIST

10.65 English composition	**10.69** biology	**10.73** world languages	**10.77** algebra
10.66 world history	**10.70** chemistry	**10.74** marching band	**10.78** geometry
10.67 U.S. history	**10.71** physics	**10.75** art history	**10.79** trigonometry
10.68 geography	**10.72** astronomy	**10.76** keyboarding	**10.80** calculus

Areas of Study

GRAMMAR ACTIVITY

Welcome to California

1. Work with 2 classmates.
2. Label what you see in the picture. Take turns.
3. Check your spelling in the *OPD*.

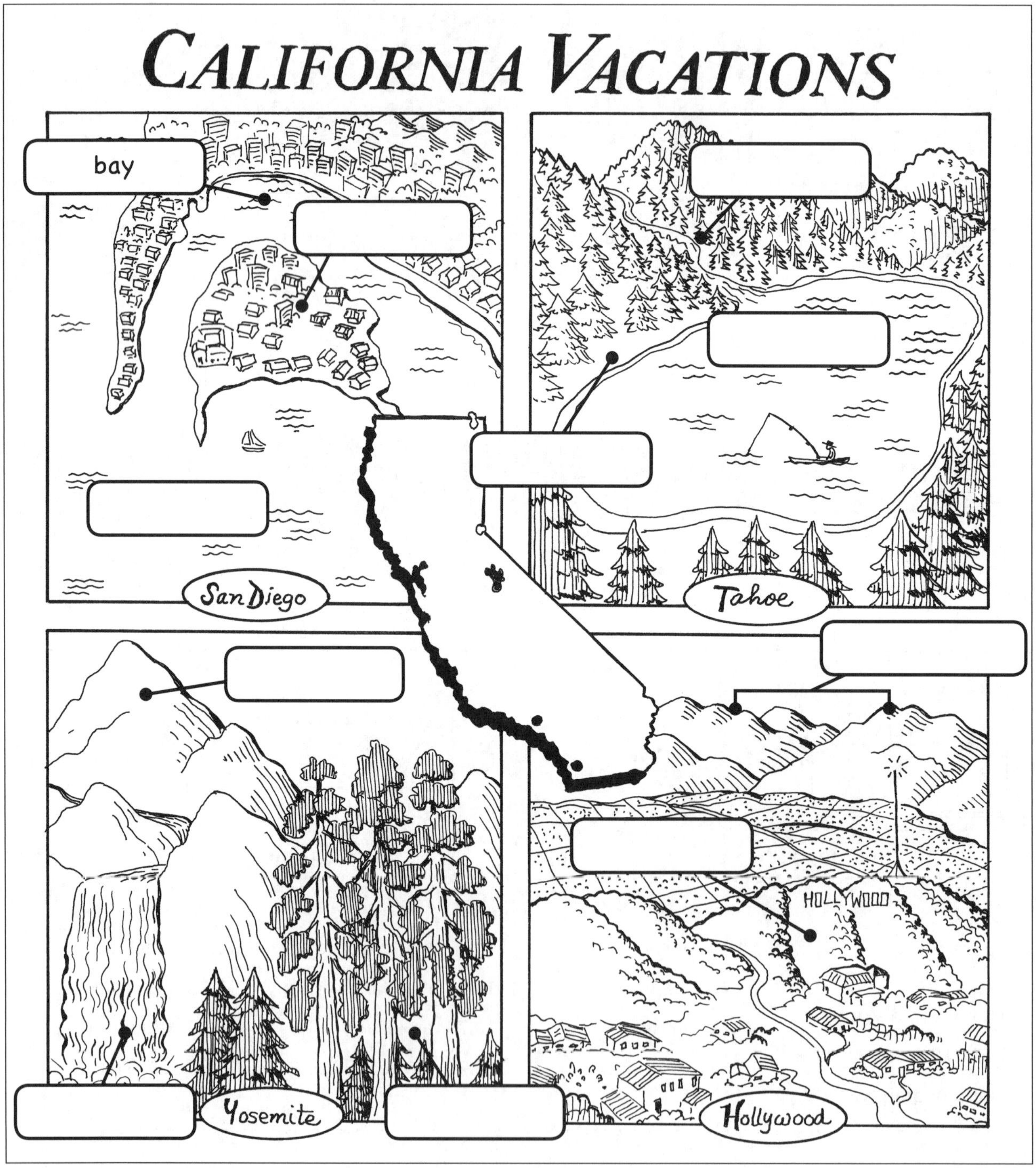

▶ **What's Next?** Continue working with your group. Pick a popular vacation place you know. Make a tourist brochure for that place. List important information and show a picture of the geography of that place. Share your brochure with the class.

In the Lab A

1. Find a partner with page 182 (B). Don't show your partner this paper.
2. Describe Picture A to your partner. Your partner will draw what you say.
3. Answer your partner's questions.

4. Listen to your partner describe Picture B. Draw what you hear. You can ask questions like these: *What's next to the _____ ? Is there a _____ ?*
5. When both pictures are complete, compare them.

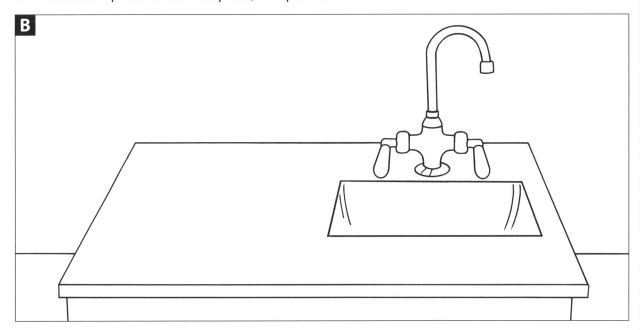

▶ **What's Next?** Do you like using the computer? How often do you use it? What do you use it for? Write five sentences and read them to your partner. Then discuss how you and your partner are the same or different.

Areas of Study

A

Areas of Study

▶ **Drawing Dictation B** (See page xviii for Teacher's Notes.)   *OPD* pages 194–196

In the Lab B

1. Find a partner with page 181 (A). Don't show your partner this paper.
2. Listen to your partner describe Picture A. Draw what you hear. You can ask questions like these: *What's next to the _____ ? Is there a _____ ?*

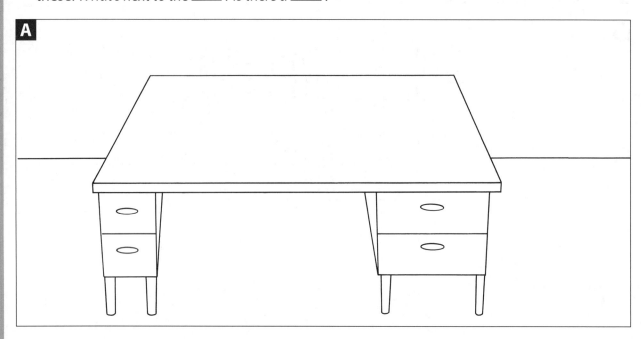

A

3. Describe Picture B to your partner. Your partner will draw what you say.
4. Answer your partner's questions.
5. When both pictures are complete, compare them.

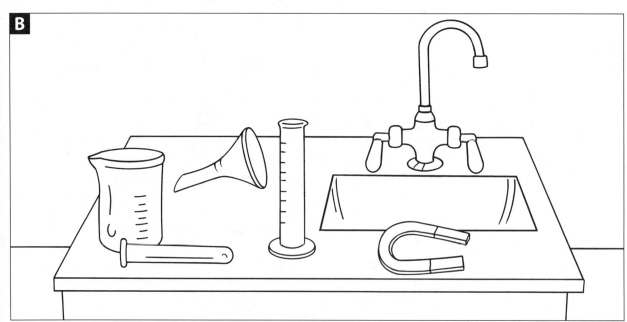

B

▶ **What's Next?** Do you like using the computer? How often do you use it? What do you use it for? Write five sentences and read them to your partner. Then discuss how you and your partner are the same or different.

B

Place

182 Unit Ten   © 2009 Oxford University Press • Permission granted to reproduce for classroom use.

Around the World

1. Work with 3 or 4 classmates. Choose a Recorder.

2. Use the cards to make 10 different sentences or questions. The Recorder writes them down.

I	YOU	HE	SHE
THEY	AM	IS	ARE
WHERE	FROM	BRAZIL	ITALY
MEXICO	VIETNAM	NIGERIA	CHINA
OR	NOT	.	?

▶ **What's Next?** Share your sentences with the class. Which group made the most sentences? the most questions?

It's so beautiful A

1. Find a partner with page 185 (B). Look at each other's picture.

2. Find 10 differences with your partner. Write the differences in the chart.

	A	B
1.	A boat is in the bay.	There is no boat in the bay.
2.		
3.		
4.		
5.		
6.		
7.		
8.		
9.		
10.		

▶ **What's Next?** Look at the places on page 204 of the *OPD*. Are any of them near where you live? Do you want to live near any of them? Why? Discuss with your partner.

It's so beautiful B

1. Find a partner with page 184 (A). Look at each other's picture.

2. Find 10 differences with your partner. Write the differences in the chart.

	A	B
1.	A boat is in the bay.	There is no boat in the bay.
2.		
3.		
4.		
5.		
6.		
7.		
8.		
9.		
10.		

▶ **What's Next?** Look at the places on page 204 of the *OPD*. Are any of them near where you live? Do you want to live near any of them? Why? Discuss with your partner.

Areas of Study

B

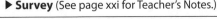

What's your favorite subject?

1. Read the questions. Mark your answers with a ✔.

2. Survey 5 classmates. Write their names, and mark their answers with a ✔.

Which do you like to study more?	My answers	_____ answers	_____ answers	_____ answers	_____ answers	_____ answers
Math **OR** language arts?						
World history **OR** U.S. history?						
Algebra **OR** geometry?						
Biology **OR** Chemistry?						
Art **OR** music?						
Ancient civilizations **OR** modern civilizations?						
World languages **OR** ESL?						

3. Write sentences about each classmate you surveyed.

Ben likes to study language arts more than math.

1. _____

2. _____

3. _____

4. _____

5. _____

4. Work with 2 classmates. Read your sentences out loud and compare them.

▶ **What's Next?** Write sentences about your answers.

A Busy Day at School

1. Work with 2 classmates.

2. Look at the pictures. Read the first sentence. Think of more sentences to write about the pictures.

3. Take turns writing sentences to continue the story.

4. Check your spelling in the *OPD*.

Ming had a busy day at school yesterday.

_____

_____

_____

_____

_____

_____

_____

_____

▶ **What's Next?** What did you learn at school last week? Write sentences and read them to a classmate.

Areas of Study

Areas of Study

Explorers and Inventors A

1. Find a partner with page 189 (B). Don't show your partner this paper.
2. Look at A. Ask your partner about the missing information in this chart. You can ask questions like these: *What area did ____ explore? When did ____ explore ____ ?*
3. Write the missing information.

A

AMAZING DISCOVERIES

EXPLORER	AREA EXPLORED	DATE	COUNTRY
Christopher Columbus	West Indies	_____	Italy
Ponce de Leon	_____	1513	_____
Francisco Coronado	_____	_____	Spain
Samuel de Champlain	Maine	_____	_____
Henry Hudson	_____	1610	United Kingdom
Vitus Bering	_____	1741	_____
Robert Peary	_____	1892	_____

A

4. Look at B. Use this chart to answer your partner's questions.
5. When you are finished, compare your charts with your partner's.

B

INCREDIBLE INVENTIONS

INVENTOR	INVENTION	DATE	COUNTRY
Alexander Graham Bell	telephone	1876	U.S.A.
Thomas Edison	light bulb	1879	U.S.A.
Karl Benz	car	1885	Germany
Guglielmo Marconi	radio	1895	Italy
John Baird	TV	1926	United Kingdom
Konrad Zuse	computer	1941	Germany
Tim Berners-Lee	World Wide Web	1989	United Kingdom

▶ **What's Next?** Continue working with your partner. Use the maps on pages 200–203 of the *OPD* to locate the places in the charts.

Areas of Study

Explorers and Inventors B

1. Find a partner with page 188 (A). Don't show your partner this paper.
2. Look at A. Use this chart to answer your partner's questions.

A

AMAZING DISCOVERIES

EXPLORER	AREA EXPLORED	DATE	COUNTRY
Christopher Columbus	West Indies	1492	Italy
Ponce de Leon	Florida	1513	Spain
Francisco Coronado	Southwest U.S.A.	1540 – 1542	Spain
Samuel de Champlain	Maine	1604	France
Henry Hudson	Canada	1610	United Kingdom
Vitus Bering	Alaska	1741	Denmark
Robert Peary	Greenland	1892	U.S.A.

3. Look at B. Ask your partner about the missing information in this chart. You can ask questions like these: *What did _____ invent? When did _____ invent it? Where was _____ from?*
4. Write the missing information.
5. When you are finished, compare your charts with your partner's.

B

B

INCREDIBLE INVENTIONS

INVENTOR	INVENTION	DATE	COUNTRY
Alexander Graham Bell	telephone	_____	_____
Thomas Edison	_____	_____	U.S.A.
Karl Benz	_____	1885	_____
Guglielmo Marconi	radio	_____	_____
John Baird	_____	1926	_____
Konrad Zuse	_____	_____	Germany
Tim Berners-Lee	World Wide Web	_____	_____

▶ **What's Next?** Continue working with your partner. Use the maps on pages 200–203 of the *OPD* to locate the places in the charts.

Time for Class

1. Work with 2 classmates.

2. Write the character next to each line.

3. Choose your character. Write other lines you could say.

4. Practice saying the lines. Act out the role play.

The Scene

a classroom where
English composition
is being taught

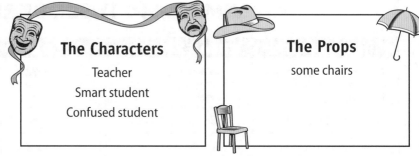

The Characters

Teacher
Smart student
Confused student

The Props

some chairs

The Script

Teacher:	Class, can you tell me some punctuation you know?
	I know that a period* goes at the end of a sentence.
	Huh? I don't understand. Can you explain periods again?
	We use periods at the end of sentences and for abbreviations.
	Oh, OK. I think I understand.
	What about question marks? Can someone explain them?
	I can! Question marks are used at the end of questions.
	That's correct. How about another punctuation mark?
	I think I can explain exclamation marks. They are used at the
	beginning and end of sentences to show strong feelings.
	That's almost right but not quite.

*You can use other vocabulary for the underlined words.

▶ **What's Next?** Write a paragraph about your favorite school subject. Try to use all of the punctuation on page 190 of the *OPD*. Read and show your paragraph to a classmate.

Space Exploration—Yes or No?

1. Think about reasons to explore space or not to explore space.
2. Read the statements in the chart.
3. Write 2 more statements in the chart.
4. If the statement shows that space exploration is a good idea, ✔ that column. If the statement shows that space exploration is a bad idea, ✔ that column.

Statements	good idea	bad idea
Scientists can study other planets in our solar system.		
Scientists can do experiments in space.		
Space exploration costs a lot of money.		
Countries that explore space are respected by other countries.		
Many new inventions are created because of space exploration.		
Space exploration creates a lot of trash in space.		
Space exploration could allow people to move to other planets one day.		
From space, scientists can learn more about problems on Earth.		
Space exploration can be very dangerous.		
Countries may not use space exploration peacefully.		

5. Work with a partner. Compare your ideas.
6. Write your and your partner's ideas.

I think that space exploration is a _____ idea because _____

_____

My partner thinks that space exploration is a _____ idea because _____

_____

▶ **What's Next?** Work as a class. How many students think space exploration is a good idea? a bad idea? Draw a bar graph on the board. Then discuss the results.

       Unit Ten   **191**

Areas of Study

Animals Who Like Water

1. Work with a partner. Cut apart the cards.
2. Write the Word List words on the back of the cards.
3. Student A: Show the picture to your partner.
   Student B: Say the word or phrase.
4. Take turns.

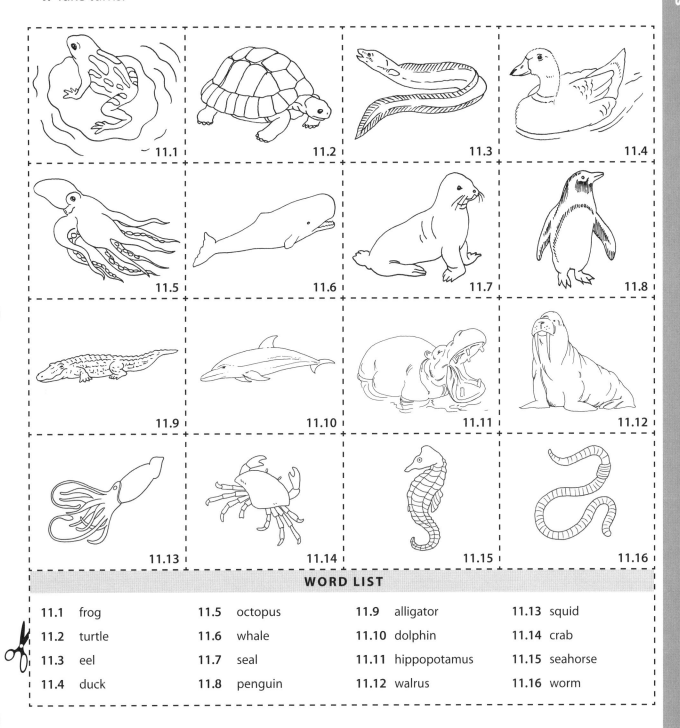

WORD LIST			
11.1 frog	**11.5** octopus	**11.9** alligator	**11.13** squid
11.2 turtle	**11.6** whale	**11.10** dolphin	**11.14** crab
11.3 eel	**11.7** seal	**11.11** hippopotamus	**11.15** seahorse
11.4 duck	**11.8** penguin	**11.12** walrus	**11.16** worm

Birds with Feathers, Animals with Fur

1. Work with a partner. Cut apart the cards.

2. Write the Word List words on the back of the cards.

3. Student A: Show the picture to your partner.
　　 Student B: Say the word or phrase.

4. Take turns.

11.17	11.18	11.19	11.20
11.21	11.22	11.23	11.24
11.25	11.26	11.27	11.28
11.29	11.30	11.31	11.32

WORD LIST

11.17 cat	11.21 coyote	11.25 leopard	11.29 peacock
11.18 rabbit	11.22 squirrel	11.26 panda	11.30 sparrow
11.19 mouse	11.23 chipmunk	11.27 bat	11.31 parakeet
11.20 tiger	11.24 koala	11.28 owl	11.32 rooster

What am I?

1. Work with 3 classmates. Cut apart the cards. Put them face down in a pile.
2. Student A: Pick a card. Describe the word or phrase on the card.
   Students B, C, and D: Guess the word or phrase.
3. The first student to guess correctly keeps the card.
4. Take turns.

WORD LIST

11.33 horse	**11.37** cow	**11.41** llama	**11.45** daisy
11.34 sheep	**11.38** honeybee	**11.42** monkey	**11.46** rose
11.35 goat	**11.39** deer	**11.43** zebra	**11.47** pine tree
11.36 pig	**11.40** gorilla	**11.44** lizard	**11.48** palm tree

Plants and Animals

What do I have?

1. Work with 3 classmates. Cut apart the cards. Put them face down in a pile.
2. Student A: Pick a card. Describe the word or phrase on the card.
   Students B, C, and D: Guess the word or phrase.
3. The first student to guess correctly keeps the card.
4. Take turns.

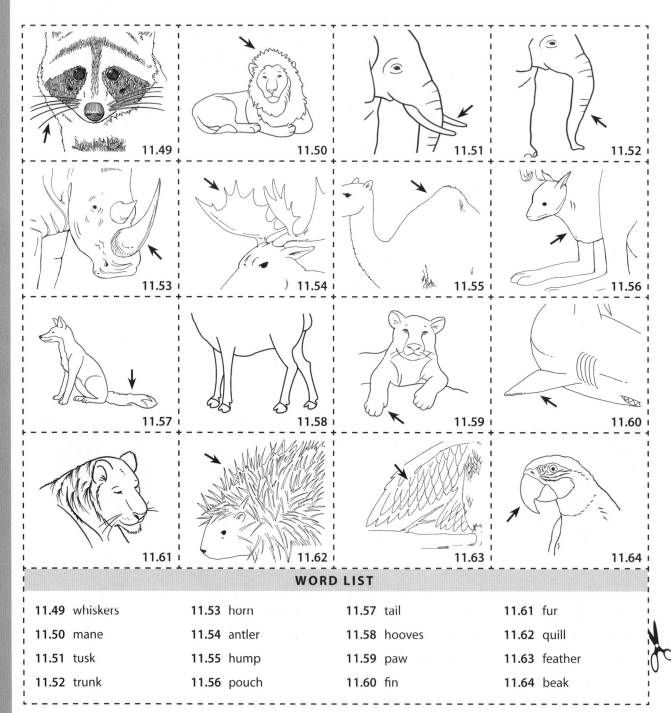

WORD LIST			
11.49 whiskers	11.53 horn	11.57 tail	11.61 fur
11.50 mane	11.54 antler	11.58 hooves	11.62 quill
11.51 tusk	11.55 hump	11.59 paw	11.63 feather
11.52 trunk	11.56 pouch	11.60 fin	11.64 beak

Wild Animals Grid

1. Use this grid with the picture cards on page 198.

2. Student A: Put one picture on each square on the grid. Don't show your partner your grid.

Use the picture and the square to tell your partner a sentence.

(*I see a big moose.*)

Student B: Listen to your partner. Check what you heard.

(*Did you say you see a big moose?*)

Put the picture on the correct square on the grid.

3. When the grids are full, compare them. If they are the same, change roles. If not, try again.

big	small	friendly	quiet
noisy	dangerous	fast	slow
ugly	beautiful	soft	heavy
young	wild	tall	fat

Plants and Animals

GRAMMAR ACTIVITY

Wild Animals Cards

1. Use these picture cards with the grid on page 197.
2. Work with a partner. Cut apart the cards.

WORD LIST

11.65 moose	**11.69** elephant	**11.73** camel	**11.77** giraffe
11.66 raccoon	**11.70** rhinoceros	**11.74** goldfish	**11.78** grasshopper
11.67 dog	**11.71** lion	**11.75** shark	**11.79** eagle
11.68 porcupine	**11.72** kangaroo	**11.76** snake	**11.80** bear

Working at the Nature Center

1. Work with 2 classmates.
2. Label what you see in the picture. Take turns.
3. Check your spelling in the *OPD*.

seed

▶ **What's Next?** Draw a picture of a garden that you want to have. Which plants and flowers did you include? Tell a classmate about your garden.

A

Places to Go A

1. Find a partner with page 201 (B). Don't show your partner this paper.
2. Describe Picture A to your partner. Your partner will draw what you say.
3. Answer your partner's questions.

A

4. Listen to your partner describe Picture B. Draw what you hear. You can ask questions like these: *How many _____ are there? What kind of _____ are there?*
5. When both pictures are complete, compare them.

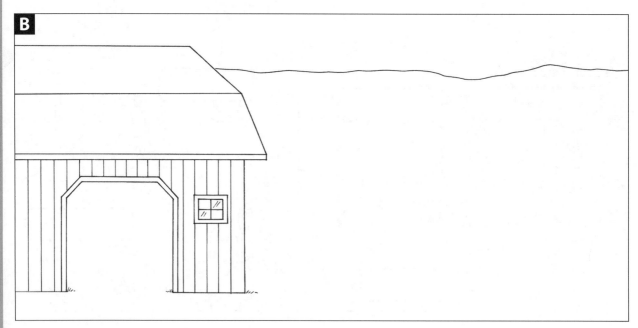

B

▶ **What's Next?** Continue working with your partner. You live on a farm. What animals do you have? Why? Discuss with your partner. Then write five sentences each about your farm and the animals you have.

Places to Go B

1. Find a partner with page 200 (A). Don't show your partner this paper.
2. Listen to your partner describe Picture A. Draw what you hear. You can ask questions like these: *How many _____ are there? What kind of _____ are there?*

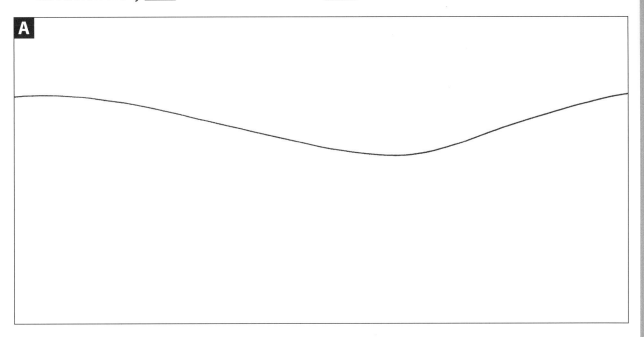

3. Describe Picture B to your partner. Your partner will draw what you say.
4. Answer your partner's questions.
5. When both pictures are complete, compare them.

B

▶ **What's Next?** Continue working with your partner. You live on a farm. What animals do you have? Why? Discuss with your partner. Then write five sentences each about your farm and the animals you have.

Conservation

1. Work with 3 or 4 classmates. Choose a Recorder.

2. Use the cards to make 10 different sentences or questions. The Recorder writes them down.

I	HE	SHE	'D
WOULD	WOULDN'T	LIKE	TO
CONSERVE	ENERGY	WATER	REDUCE
POLLUTION	WASTE	USE	NUCLEAR
SOLAR	COAL	.	?

▶ **What's Next?** Share your sentences with the class. Which group made the most sentences? the most questions?

Under the Sea A

1. Find a partner with page 204 (B). Look at each other's picture.

2. Find 10 differences with your partner. Write the differences in the chart.

A	B
1. There is one swordfish.	There are two swordfish.
2.	
3.	
4.	
5.	
6.	
7.	
8.	
9.	
10.	

▶ **What's Next?** Continue working with your partner. Which amphibians and reptiles do you want to see at an aquarium or a zoo? Why? Talk to your partner about the animals.

Under the Sea B

1. Find a partner with page 203 (A). Look at each other's picture.
2. Find 10 differences with your partner. Write the differences in the chart.

	A	B
1.	There is one swordfish.	There are two swordfish.
2.		
3.		
4.		
5.		
6.		
7.		
8.		
9.		
10.		

▶ **What's Next?** Continue working with your partner. Which amphibians and reptiles do you want to see at an aquarium or a zoo? Why? Talk to your partner about the animals.

Pets for Sale

1. Read the questions. Mark your answers with a ✔.

2. Survey 5 classmates. Write their names, and mark their answers with a ✔.

Do you prefer a ...	My answers	_____ answers	_____ answers	_____ answers	_____ answers	_____ answers
kitten **OR** puppy?						
rabbit **OR** guinea pig?						
goldfish **OR** frog?						
snake **OR** lizard?						
parakeet **OR** turtle?						
spider **OR** scorpion?						
mouse **OR** rat?						

3. Write sentences about each classmate you surveyed.

   Carol prefers a kitten to a puppy.

   1. _____

   2. _____

   3. _____

   4. _____

   5. _____

4. Work with 2 classmates. Read your sentences out loud and compare them.

▶ **What's Next?** Write sentences about your answers.

I love you, Lin!

1. Work with 2 classmates.
2. Look at the picture. Read the first sentence. Think of more sentences to write about the picture.
3. Take turns writing sentences to continue the story.
4. Check your spelling in the *OPD*.

Jose wants to get a bouquet for his date with Lin.

_____

_____

_____

_____

_____

_____

_____

_____

_____

▶ **What's Next?** Make a list of the special people in your life. You can include friends and family members. What flowers do you want to send to each person for a special event? Tell a classmate about the reasons for your choices.

Plants and Animals

Choosing a Vacation A

1. Find a partner with page 208 (B). Don't show your partner this paper.
2. Look at A. Ask your partner about the missing information in these travel brochures. You can ask questions like these: *What can you see at _____? How much is _____?*
3. Write the missing information.

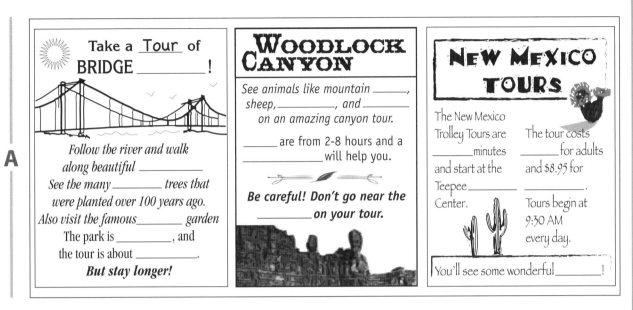

A

Take a <u>Tour</u> of BRIDGE _____!

Follow the river and walk along beautiful _____
See the many _____ trees that were planted over 100 years ago.
Also visit the famous _____ garden
The park is _____, and the tour is about _____.
But stay longer!

WOODLOCK CANYON

See animals like mountain _____, sheep, _____, and _____ on an amazing canyon tour.

_____ are from 2-8 hours and a _____ will help you.

Be careful! Don't go near the _____ on your tour.

NEW MEXICO TOURS

The New Mexico Trolley Tours are _____ minutes and start at the Teepee _____ Center.

The tour costs _____ for adults and $8.95 for _____.
Tours begin at 9:30 AM every day.

You'll see some wonderful _____!

4. Look at B. Use these travel brochures to answer your partner's questions.
5. When you are finished, compare your travel brochures with your partner's.

B

Visit the landmarks in Timson City!

Ride a bicycle along Timson City River or take a ferry down it.
Tour the caves and caverns.
Make sure you buy a gift at the new gift shop!

THE ANDANA CITY ZOO IN KILRADE IS FREE!

The zoo has a variety of animals, including elephants, gorillas, and even an octopus!

The zoo also has rare plants, flowers, and trees.

Visit every day except December 25.
Check our website for hours:
www.andanazoo.com

Oceantown is filled with wildlife and beauty.

Take a tour to see large snakes, alligators, and birds, like ducks and woodpeckers.
Fishing is a popular activity, and many types of fish can be found.

If you like the outdoors, you'll love Oceantown!

▶ **What's Next?** You are planning a vacation for you family. Which of these six landmarks or national parks would you visit? Why? Tell a classmate about your choice.

A

Choosing a Vacation B

1. Find a partner with page 207 (A). Don't show your partner this paper.
2. Look at A. Use these travel brochures to answer your partner's questions.

A

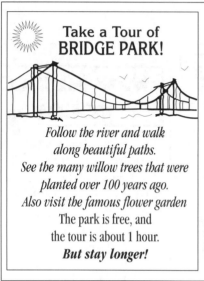

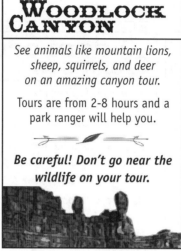

3. Look at B. Ask your partner about the missing information in these travel brochures.
You can ask questions like these: *What can you do at ____? What kind of ____ are there?*
4. Write the missing information.
5. When you are finished, compare your travel brochures with your partner's.

B

▶ **What's Next?** You are planning a vacation for you family. Which of these six
landmarks or national parks would you visit? Why? Tell a classmate about your choice.

A Day at the Zoo

1. Work with 3 classmates.

2. Write the character next to each line.

3. Choose your character. Write other lines you could say.

4. Practice saying the lines. Act out the role play.

The Scene

a parent and child at
a zoo and a gift shop

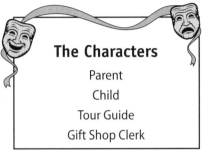

The Characters

Parent
Child
Tour Guide
Gift Shop Clerk

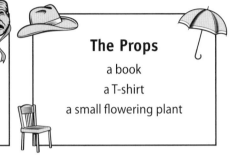

The Props

a book
a T-shirt
a small flowering plant

The Script

Child: _____ I'm learning about <u>birds</u>* in school.

_____ Well, then look at this <u>eagle</u>. Doesn't it have unusual <u>feathers</u>?

_____ You're right! What are those <u>trees</u>? Their <u>branches</u> are beautiful.

_____ Those are <u>willow trees</u>. They grow very well here.

_____ Can I pet the baby <u>llama</u>?

_____ You sure can. But be careful!

_____ Let's stop at this gift shop. Do you have books on <u>seahorses</u>?

_____ Yes, we do and all <u>marine life</u> books are <u>25%</u> off.

_____ Great! And do you have any <u>T-shirts</u>?

_____ Sure we do. Would you also like a free <u>daisy</u> plant?

_____ Ah-choo! No thanks, I'm allergic to <u>daisies</u>.

_____ _____

_____ _____

_____ _____

_____ _____

*You can use other vocabulary for the underlined words.

▶ **What's Next?** Continue working with your group. Plan a new zoo for your city. Decide which plants, animals, and special attractions you want to include. Draw a map showing your plan for the zoo and share it with the class.

Plants and Animals

Are you a dog person or a cat person?

1. Think about reasons to own a dog or to own a cat.
2. Read the statements in the chart.
3. Write 2 more statements in the chart.
4. If the statement shows that owning a dog is a good idea, ✔ that column. If the statement shows that owning a cat is a good idea, ✔ that column.

Statements	owning a dog	owning a cat
Cats can live in small apartments.		
Many dogs bark when their owners are away from home.		
You can teach a dog games or tricks, like rolling over or shaking hands.		
Cats do not eat a lot.		
Cats like to scratch their claws on furniture and doors.		
Dogs can protect your home and family.		
Cats don't need a lot of attention.		
You don't have to walk a cat.		
Dogs make good friends for lonely people.		
Walking a dog is good exercise.		

5. Work with a partner. Compare your ideas.
6. Write your and your partner's ideas.

I think that owning a _____ is a good idea because _____

_____

My partner thinks that owning a _____ is a good idea because _____

_____

▶ **What's Next?** Work as a class. How many students prefer owning a dog? owning a cat? Draw a bar graph on the board. Then discuss the results.

Where are you going?

1. Work with a partner. Cut apart the cards.

2. Write the Word List words on the back of the cards.

3. Student A: Show the picture to your partner.
   Student B: Say the word or phrase.

4. Take turns.

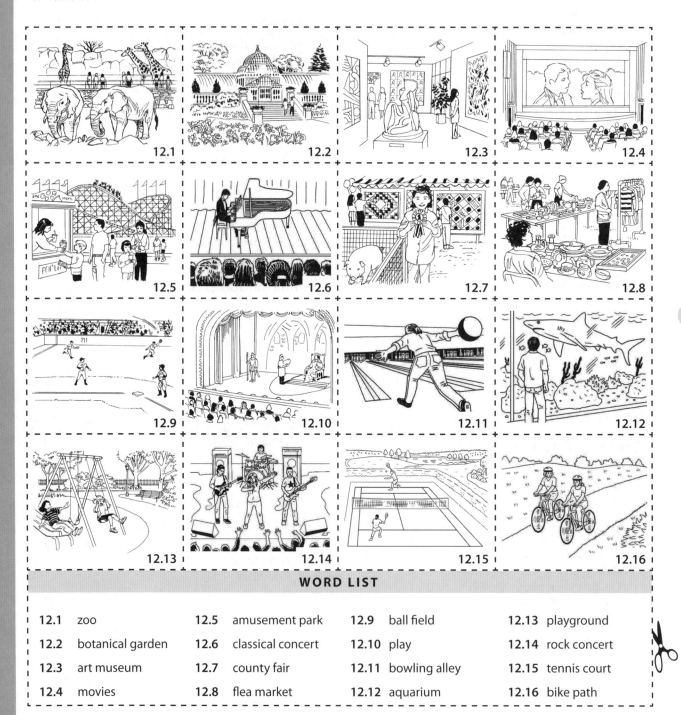

WORD LIST			
12.1 zoo	**12.5** amusement park	**12.9** ball field	**12.13** playground
12.2 botanical garden	**12.6** classical concert	**12.10** play	**12.14** rock concert
12.3 art museum	**12.7** county fair	**12.11** bowling alley	**12.15** tennis court
12.4 movies	**12.8** flea market	**12.12** aquarium	**12.16** bike path

That's my favorite hobby

1. Work with a partner. Cut apart the cards.
2. Write the Word List words on the back of the cards.
3. Student A: Show the picture to your partner.
   Student B: Say the word or phrase.
4. Take turns.

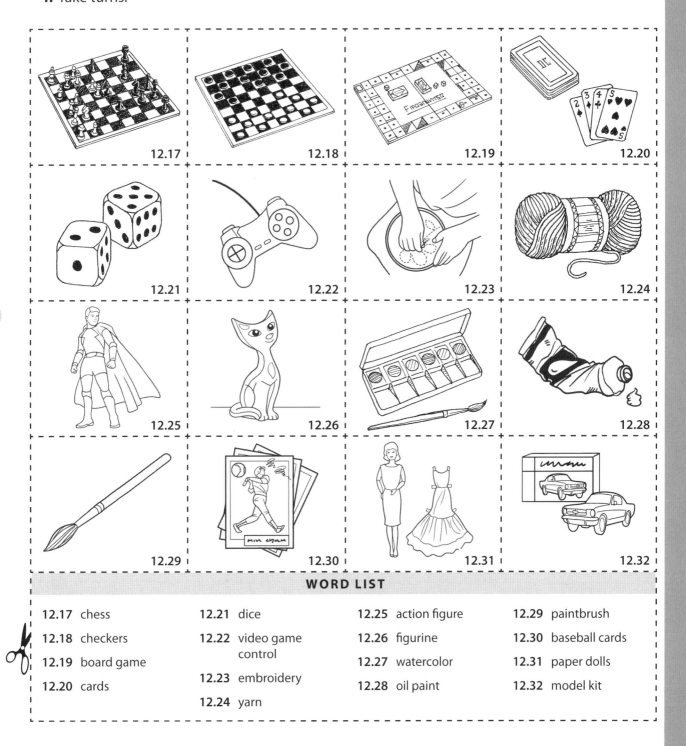

12.17	12.18	12.19	12.20
12.21	12.22	12.23	12.24
12.25	12.26	12.27	12.28
12.29	12.30	12.31	12.32

WORD LIST

12.17 chess	12.21 dice	12.25 action figure	12.29 paintbrush
12.18 checkers	12.22 video game control	12.26 figurine	12.30 baseball cards
12.19 board game	12.23 embroidery	12.27 watercolor	12.31 paper dolls
12.20 cards	12.24 yarn	12.28 oil paint	12.32 model kit

Recreation

Recreation

My Entertainment Center

1. Work with 3 classmates. Cut apart the cards. Put them face down in a pile.

2. Student A: Pick a card. Describe the word or phrase on the card.
   Students B, C, and D: Guess the word or phrase.

3. The first student to guess correctly keeps the card.

4. Take turns.

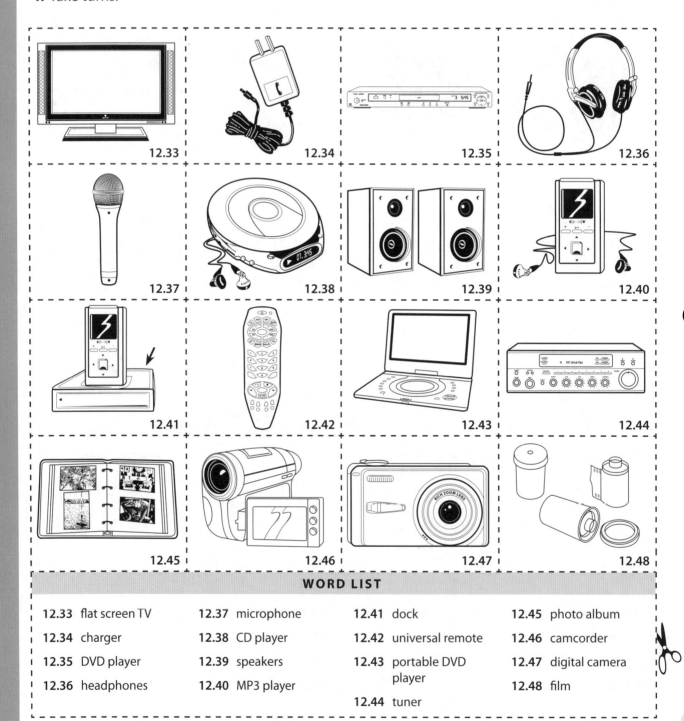

12.33	12.34	12.35	12.36
12.37	12.38	12.39	12.40
12.41	12.42	12.43	12.44
12.45	12.46	12.47	12.48

WORD LIST

12.33 flat screen TV	**12.37** microphone	**12.41** dock	**12.45** photo album
12.34 charger	**12.38** CD player	**12.42** universal remote	**12.46** camcorder
12.35 DVD player	**12.39** speakers	**12.43** portable DVD player	**12.47** digital camera
12.36 headphones	**12.40** MP3 player	**12.44** tuner	**12.48** film

Goal!

1. Work with 3 classmates. Cut apart the cards. Put the cards face down in a pile.
2. Student A: Pick a card. Silently act out the action.
   Student B: Ask *What did he / she do?*
   Students C and D: Answer the question using the past tense. (*She threw the ball.*)
   Student B: Write what your classmates say.
3. Take turns.

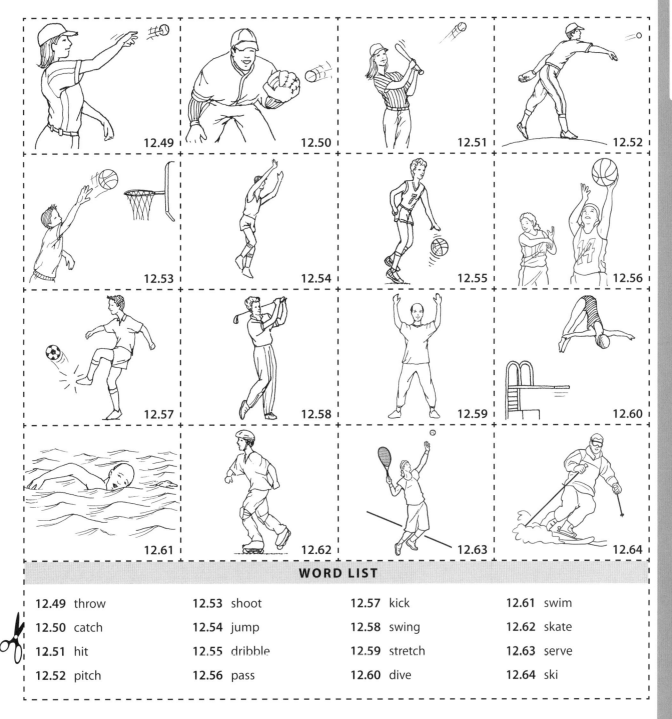

WORD LIST			
12.49 throw	**12.53** shoot	**12.57** kick	**12.61** swim
12.50 catch	**12.54** jump	**12.58** swing	**12.62** skate
12.51 hit	**12.55** dribble	**12.59** stretch	**12.63** serve
12.52 pitch	**12.56** pass	**12.60** dive	**12.64** ski

Outdoor Activities Grid

1. Use this grid with the picture cards on page 217.

2. Student A: Put one picture on each square on the grid. Don't show your partner your grid.

Use the picture and the square to tell your partner a sentence.

(*Carmen enjoys camping.*)

Student B: Listen to your partner. Check what you heard.

(*Did you say Carmen enjoys camping?*)

Put the picture on the correct square on the grid.

3. When the grids are full, compare them. If they are the same, change roles. If not, try again.

Carmen	Olivia and Nira	Andy	Vicky
Josh	Charles	Chen	Roberto and Tomas
Max	Jing-li	Lina	Mustafa
He	She	We	They

Outdoor Activities Cards

1. Use these picture cards with the grid on page 216.
2. Work with a partner. Cut apart the cards.

WORD LIST

12.65 camping	**12.69** windsurfing	**12.73** fishing	**12.77** mountain biking
12.66 sailing	**12.70** snorkeling	**12.74** hiking	**12.78** ice skating
12.67 scuba diving	**12.71** horseback riding	**12.75** backpacking	**12.79** snowboarding
12.68 surfing	**12.72** sledding	**12.76** rafting	**12.80** canoeing

Recreation / GRAMMAR ACTIVITY

A Camping Trip

1. Work with 2 classmates.
2. Label what you see in the picture. Take turns.
3. Check your spelling in the *OPD*.

matches

▶ **What's Next?** Work with a partner. You are going on a camping trip, but you can only take 6 items. Which items do you take? Take turns telling your partner about the items and why you are taking them. Share your list and reasons with the class.

On the Ball A

1. Find a partner with page 220 (B). Don't show your partner this paper.
2. Describe Picture A to your partner. Your partner will draw what you say.
3. Answer your partner's questions.

4. Listen to your partner describe Picture B. Draw what you hear. You can ask questions like these: *Where is the _____? How many _____ are there?*
5. When both pictures are complete, compare them.

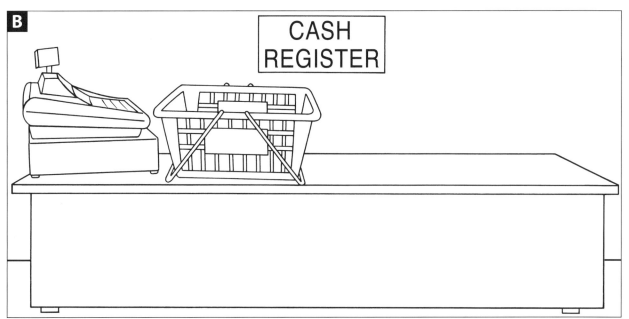

▶ **What's Next?** Work with a group. Which sports are the most popular among your group members? What equipment do you need for the sports? Make a list. Share your list with the class.

On the Ball B

1. Find a partner with page 219 (A). Don't show your partner this paper.
2. Listen to your partner describe Picture A. Draw what you hear. You can ask questions like these: *Where is the _____? How many _____ are there?*

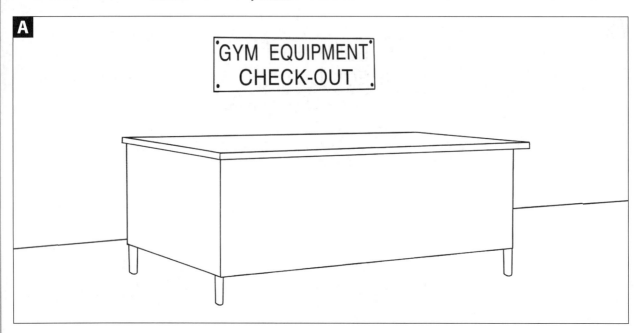

3. Describe Picture B to your partner. Your partner will draw what you say.
4. Answer your partner's questions.
5. When both pictures are complete, compare them.

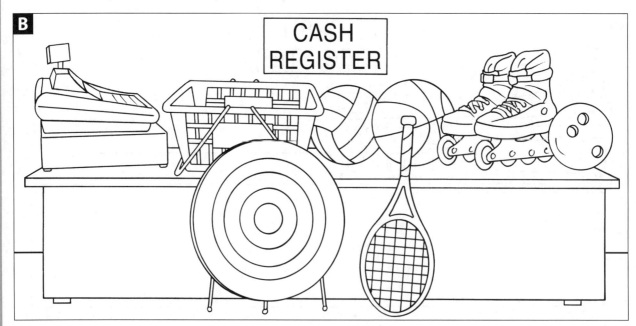

▶ **What's Next?** Work with a group. Which sports are the most popular among your group members? What equipment do you need for the sports? Make a list. Share your list with the class.

Outdoor Fun, All Year Around

1. Work with 3 or 4 classmates. Choose a Recorder.
2. Use the cards to make 10 different sentences or questions. The Recorder writes them down.

HE	SHE	WE	GOES
GO	CAMPING	HIKING	SKATING
SKIING	IN	THE	SUMMER
WINTER	WHEN	WHERE	NOT
DOES	DO	.	?

▶ **What's Next?** Share your sentences with the class. Which group made the most sentences? the most questions?

Unit Twelve   **221**

Recreation

GRAMMAR ACTIVITY

A Day at the Beach A

1. Find a partner with page 223 (B). Look at each other's picture.

2. Find 10 differences with your partner. Write the differences in the chart.

	A		**B**
1.	The sailboat's sail is down.		The sailboat's sail is up.
2.			
3.			
4.			
5.			
6.			
7.			
8.			
9.			
10.			

▶ **What's Next?** Continue working with your partner. You are going to the beach together. What will you take? Make a list and share it with the class.

A Day at the Beach B

1. Find a partner with page 222 (A). Look at each other's picture.

2. Find 10 differences with your partner. Write the differences in the chart.

	A	B
1.	The sailboat's sail is down.	The sailboat's sail is up.
2.		
3.		
4.		
5.		
6.		
7.		
8.		
9.		
10.		

▶ **What's Next?** Continue working with your partner. You are going to the beach together. What will you take? Make a list and share it with the class.

What do you want to do?

1. Read the questions. Mark your answers with a ✔.

2. Survey 5 classmates. Write their names, and mark their answer with a ✔.

Which is better ...	My answers	_____ answers	_____ answers	_____ answers	_____ answers	_____ answers
playing a video game **OR** playing a board game?						
watching a comedy **OR** watching a romance?						
watching a game show **OR** watching a soap opera?						
listening to a CD player **OR** listening to an MP3 player?						
using a digital camera **OR** using a film camera?						
playing cards **OR** watching TV?						

3. Write sentences about each classmate you surveyed.

Tim thinks playing a video game is better than playing a board game.

1. _____

2. _____

3. _____

4. _____

5. _____

4. Work with 2 classmates. Read your sentences out loud and compare them.

▶ **What's Next?** Write sentences about your answers.

Recreation

GRAMMAR ACTIVITY

A Fun Saturday

1. Work with 2 classmates.
2. Look at the pictures. Read the first sentence. Think of more sentences to write about the pictures.
3. Take turns writing sentences to continue the story.
4. Check your spelling in the *OPD*.

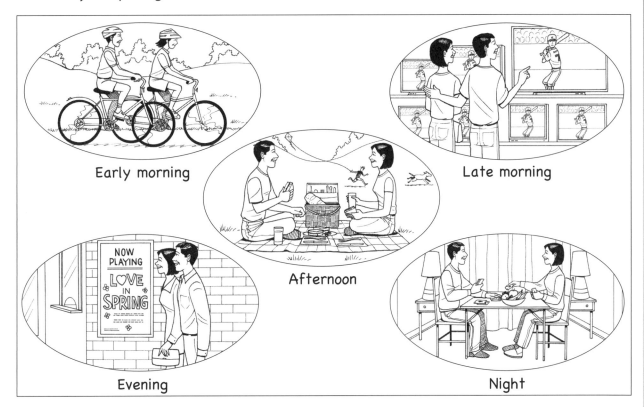

Early morning

Late morning

Afternoon

Evening

Night

Alberto and Selena had a lot of fun last Saturday.

_____

_____

_____

_____

_____

_____

_____

_____

▶ **What's Next?** What did you do last Saturday? Write five sentences. Share your sentences with the class.

Coming Up in Los Angeles A

1. Find a partner with page 227 (B). Don't show your partner this paper.

2. Look at A. Ask your partner about the missing information in this calendar of events. You can ask questions like these: *What is happening at _____ ? What time does _____ open?*

3. Write the missing information.

A

4. Look at B. Use this calendar of events to answer your partner's questions.

5. When you are finished, compare your calendars with your partner's.

A

B

▶ **What's Next?** Make a list of places you want to visit in your city or a city you know. Why do you want to visit the places? Tell a classmate about them and your reasons for visiting.

Coming Up in Los Angeles B

1. Find a partner with page 226 (A). Don't show your partner this paper.

2. Look at A. Use this calendar of events to answer your partner's questions.

A

3. Look at B. Ask your partner about the missing information in this calendar of events. You can ask questions like these: *What is happening at _____? When is the _____?*

4. Write the missing information.

5. When you are finished, compare your calendars with your partner's.

B

B

▶ **What's Next?** Make a list of places you want to visit in your city or a city you know. Why do you want to visit the places? Tell a classmate about them and your reasons for visiting.

Recreation

So Many Programs, So Many Choices!

1. Work with 2 classmates.
2. Write the character next to each line.
3. Choose your character. Write other lines you could say.
4. Practice saying the lines. Act out the role play.

The Scene

a living room in a home
with only one
TV set

The Characters

Parent
Teenager
Child

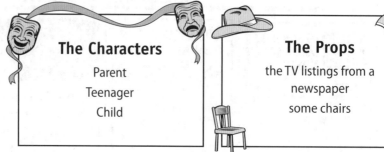

The Props

the TV listings from a
newspaper
some chairs

The Script

Parent:	OK, everyone, what should we watch tonight?
	I think there's a good cartoon* on tonight.
	No, let's watch Horror Theater!
	I'm scared of Horror Theater!
	Well, how about this? It looks like a good game show.
	No way! Let's watch this new reality show at 8:00.
	I hate reality shows. Please, let's watch the cartoon!
	Cartoons are silly and boring.
	Check the sports listings. Maybe a good game is on tonight.
	There's a soccer game on in a few minutes.
	Let's watch that!

*You can use other vocabulary for the underlined words.

▶ **What's Next?** Continue working with your group. What happens when people in your home want to watch different TV programs? How do you solve the problem? Tell your group.

Celebrate Holidays in Large or Small Groups?

1. Think about reasons to celebrate holidays in a large group or in a small group.
2. Read the statements in the chart.
3. Write 2 more statements in the chart.
4. If the statement shows that celebrating holidays in a large group is a good idea, ✔ that column. If the statement shows that celebrating holidays in small group is a good idea, ✔ that column.

Statements	large group	small group
You have to spend a lot of time preparing for visitors.		
You can have a quiet and relaxed time.		
You can go places or see things (like a parade) easily .		
You can talk to people you haven't seen in a long time.		
You can play fun games and sports that need many players.		
Children with have others to play with.		
You won't have enough time to talk to everyone.		
You can ask people to help you prepare.		
You will need to spend more money.		
It will be easy to clean up after the holiday.		

5. Work with a partner. Compare your ideas.
6. Write your and your partner's ideas.

I think that celebrating holidays in a _____ group is a good idea because
_____

My partner thinks that celebrating holidays in a _____ group is a good idea because _____

▶ **What's Next?** Take a stand. Your teacher will tell you where to stand if you think celebrating holidays in large groups is a good idea and where to stand if you think celebrating holidays in small groups is a good idea.

Activity Index